GOD HATH MADE ME TO LAUGH

Kathleen Lawrence-Smith

BY THE SAME AUTHOR

The Bassano Tragedy
Laugh with Me

ABOUT THE AUTHOR

Kathleen Lawrence-Smith has lived in Worcester all her life, with the exception of the war years, the early nineteen forties, though she is quite widely travelled, having toured much of Europe and crossed the U.S.A. and Canada twice. Tracing and retreading historical routes is part of the attraction of travel for her, as is evidenced in her writing, though with a lively interpretation of the past.

This writer is a suburban housewife and mother whose interests in the world around are widened by her family's involvement in property development and more particularly in the area of tenant/landlord relationships, some of which form the basis of entertaining anecdotes.

Mrs Lawrence-Smith's Christian philosophy is inevitably mirrored in her experiences and writing. Though herself an evangelical, she has a marked tolerance for those with differing views, which probably accounts for her considerable interest in interdenominational movements such as those featuring Billy Graham. She supports her husband in his involvement with the Full Gospel Businessmen's Fellowship International, featuring dinner meetings and similar functions - and entertaining speakers on quite a large scale.

Her writing experience in earlier years was confined to freelance work for the press and magazines. Taking over editorship of a small religious quarterly in 1972 (which has since trebled its circulation in Britain and overseas) took precedence for some years, particularly as she and her husband were engaged in the distribution of it.

The couple have two sons in business, one daughter at home and two small, lively grandsons, and are very conscious of the value of family life.

God Hath Made Me To Laugh

A Worcester Childhood

by

KATHLEEN LAWRENCE-SMITH

An autobiographical story of life
between the wars in Worcester

BRIDGE
PUBLICATIONS

PENISTONE · ENGLAND

Bridge Publications
2 Bridge Street, Penistone
Sheffield S30 6AJ

First Published 1984
Reprinted 1987

Cover Picture: WORCESTER CATHEDRAL by Bruce Freeman

British Library Cataloguing in Publication Data

Lawrence-Smith, Kathleen
    God hath made me to laugh.
    1. Worcester (Hereford and Worcester) —
    Social life and customs
    I. Title
    942.4'48083   DA670.W9

    ISBN 0-947934-00-6

Printed and Bound in Great Britain by
Whitstable Litho Ltd., Whitstable, Kent

From: The Rt. Hon. Peter Walker, M.B.E., M.P.

HOUSE OF COMMONS

Worcester is very much a microcosm of England. As a City
it has played an important role in history. It possesses
one of the most beautiful cathedrals in the country. It is
surrounded by what can only be described as typical English
countryside, and it sits astride one of Britain's greatest
rivers.

Above all Worcester is a community, and it is a community
which shares the experiences of Britain as a whole; the
industrial revolution; the emergence of the motorcar; the
social and economic changes.

It is good therefore that Kathleen Lawrence-Smith, who has
lived her life in this city, should with skill and with humour
put her pen to paper and describe the experiences she has
witnessed living in its centre. It is a book to be enjoyed,
not just by those who know the city well, but by those who,
after reading it, will decide that a visit to the City of
Worcester is a must.

Acknowledgments

I gladly express my appreciation to those who encouraged
this production – my husband, Ray, for his patient accep-
tance of having 'married the family', my cousins of the Hardwick line, Jo Freeman and Monica Radburn for their unflag-
ging interest, and the Worcester Writers Circle for electing
me to their fraternity on the strength of its early chapters.
The following artists contributed their skills to the por-
trayal of characters and situations in the story: Mr Ernest
Wellesbury ('Grandfather Lawrence' and No 3 Friar Street),
Mr Bruce Freeman ('To Market' and 'Choir Concert') and
Mrs Pat Hughes produced all the other original sketches.
For permission to reproduce published sketches of Tudor
House, Greyfriars, King Charles' House and Edgar Tower I
am indebted to the Curator of Worcester Museum and Art
Gallery; for 'St Nicholas Church' to Mrs Janet Mills, and for
'Powick Bridge' (by the late Frank Rayer) to Harold and
Gladys Bradley, editors of Worcester Anthology '71.
The photograph of Worcester Cathedral was taken by
my nephew John Lawrence; Canal Boats by Keith Ferguson;
those of Browning's Shop and Wall's Bakery were kindly
loaned by the respective families. I sought in vain for one
or two possible copyright holders and if I have inadvertently
trespassed in this regard, I trust I may be forgiven and
allowed to rectify matters where possible.
Finally, my title is taken from the book of Genesis, chapter 21, verse 6, and to the Author of that Book I owe an
eternal debt.

KATHLEEN LAWRENCE-SMITH

The Old Coach House
Whittington
Worcester   January 1987

Contents

Illustrations

Tudor House

CHAPTER 1

Midnight Reflections

THE CATHEDRAL CHIMES boomed out a dozen times and I counted every stroke. The first one had wakened me from a light sleep in unaccustomed surroundings. Cautiously, in the ensuing silence, I opened an eye, the one that was not buried in the pillow, and was surprised to encounter flickering shadows on the bedroom wall. Kit was still awake on the other half of the big bed, propped up on one elbow and reading by the small light of her candle. I felt quickly reassured, though not a bit like going to sleep again. Sleeping was such a waste of time. I guess that's how Kit felt, too.

Kit was my father's only sister, but I never thought of her as an aunt, then or since. She was all of ten years my senior, but there was a link between us that went far to bridge that gap. I was sorry, of course, about my mother being so ill, but it was good to be here with Kit. There was a comforting warmth about her. She had time for you, which was important when a new baby had arrived and there were three of you already. I was the first and had begun to reckon it a doubtful distinction, especially in a girl. Here, with Kit, none of that mattered so much.

They had called me Kathleen after her. Secretly I would have liked a more novel name (like my sister Naomi's, for instance), but if I had to have a namesake around there wasn't anybody I would have preferred to Kit. It was my mother who called her 'Kit' and, of all the derivations there may be of our shared name, that one seemed to convey the right mixture of affection and protection we felt towards her, for although Kit and I had a lot in common, I had the advantage of a pair of good and useful legs while hers were spoiled by polio and needed the support of calipers. Which was why, when the little dormer window began to rattle, I knew it was up to me to do something about it.

'I'll fix it,' I volunteered in a low voice, and so betrayed the fact of my wakefulness to Kit. Surprised, she twisted backwards towards me and squeezed my emerging arm as I raised the bedclothes stealthily. It must have been the lateness of the hour which promoted our conspiratorial air; the rest of the house was eerily quiet, and we both knew that Grandmother was not very happy about lighted candles and bedclothes being in close proximity. This was a bit unreasonable of her, I ruminated as I slipped out of bed, for you can't read small print if your candle is on the other side of the room. I tiptoed across to the window.

Wrestling with the catch I pressed close to the pane and peered down into the dark street two storeys below. The yellow gaslight of the street lamp did little to illuminate the scene but my eye caught a movement on the pavement opposite. Two figures had emerged from the covered entry beside Tudor House, lingered for a few seconds only, and parted. The one, who appeared to be a bulky figure, was adjusting a scarf around his neck and seemed to be steadying a hard hat against the wind as he passed below the lamp towards a vehicle of some sort in the shadows. The second figure stepped back into the shadow of the entry and I was surprised to see a shirt sleeve swing against the light before he disappeared, for it was a cold night and it seemed odd for somebody to be out and about in indoor clothing.

It was quiet and still now. The vehicle had rumbled away and both men were lost to view. As my eye travelled upwards over the building opposite to us, the areas of white plaster framed by black oak beams were now clearly discernible on the face of Tudor House despite the poor street lighting. Tonight the building held an air of mystery I had not noticed in the daylight when it served as a school dental clinic with patients coming and going at regular intervals. I had watched them with some trepidation from inside Grandfather's shop window on the previous day, small faces registering varying degrees of apprehension as they arrived, and nothing whatever as they left, shrouded by scarf or handkerchief. Yet Tudor House held nothing of mystery then.

Now, in the quiet darkness, its daytime function seemed unreal and remote. Behind the latticed panes opposite to us some Elizabethan family must have called this place home. Or maybe it had been a tavern? (such a warm, comforting word compared with our twentieth century 'pub'). It was big enough for such a purpose, I was sure. Even so, in Tudor times somebody quite important would have slept in that main bedroom - snuggled away within a four-poster perhaps?

Staring across now at the uncurtained windows I began to feel a curiosity about the place and resolved to further my slight acquaintance with Stella, the caretaker's daughter. Stella's mother had shown some interest in my arrival at my grandparents, and suggested I might like to go across and play with Stella sometimes. Hitherto I had treated the invitation a little coolly, for Stella was a year or two younger than I was and somewhat pale and quiet. Now that there appeared to be attractions and interests over the road beyond hopscotch and rounders, I made the quite blatant resolve to further my opportunities without delay. 'Who knows,' I mused, 'there might even be a ghost ... or two?'

'Come back in, Pet, you'll get frozen over there.' Kit's lowered admonition from the bed broke into my thoughts and recalled me to the present. Kit was right, I realized, as I gave a final tug at the windowcatch. This was a

January night with patches of mist beyond the rooftops, and quickly now I recrossed the room and joined Kit as she hunched the bedcovers more closely around her shoulders and mine. She gave me a reassuring squeeze and bent over her book again despite the lateness of the hour.

Was this, I wondered, the Midnight Hour? The hour when everything changed ... when toy soldiers came to life and marched and drilled to perfection instead of lying imprisoned within their cardboard boxes ... the bewitched hour when dolls and golliwogs came to life and argued with teddies and other stuffed animals about the habits of their owners, usually much to their detriment. The hour when Cinderella was forced to fly back to her rags and cinders, for otherwise her beautiful finery would have faded into the drab hand-me-downs of her everyday life; her dainty shoes would have turned into clumsy clogs. She would have been shamed and humbled before that great dancing crowd at the Prince's Ball. The very thought of it made me tremble beneath the blankets. Ignominy (I had stumbled across the word quite recently), ignominy was harder to bear than anything, even pain I thought. Pain would get better some time, with or without treatment, but for ignominy I could think of no remedy.

Anyway, why was I worrying? Cinderella had tripped away double quick on the first stroke of twelve. How she had done so, in glass slippers, I could scarcely imagine. No wonder she had lost one on the stairs. She must surely have had the sense to take the other one off too as she fled, or her flight back to the kitchen would have been extremely hazardous.

She had no choice, of course. You didn't defy the orders of Fairy Godmothers. You couldn't afford to. They did not come that easily. 'I wish I had one,' I mused, snuggling my back closer to Kit's, but a little warning note at the back of my mind suggested you had to have some sort of misfortune to merit one - like having Wicked Stepsisters or some Bad Fairy issuing dire predictions of woe to come, over your cradle. 'Anyway,' my conscience told me, 'if anybody should have a Fairy Godmother it ought to be Kit,' always supposing there was such a thing, which I didn't really believe.

Meanwhile Kit seemed to be getting along pretty well without one, for her body began to tremble with suppressed laughter at whatever it was she was reading and, as she was so much heavier than I was, this had a disconcerting effect. Nevertheless I hoped she could contain her mirth, for Grandmother on the floor below did not approve of nocturnal browsings. Often, in the midst of an absorbing tale, Kit would be brought sharply back to earth by a peremptory call of 'Kate!', for sometimes the flickering shadow cast by her candle across the top landing gave Kit away. Quickly and diplomatically Kit would snuff out the little yellow flame and subside silently on to her pillow until it seemed safe to stealthily venture another match.

I rarely saw Grandmother smile when I was a child. Later I came to the conclusion that she did not suffer fools gladly and was none too impressed with the rest of humanity. Perhaps it was what happened to Kit that made her disenchanted. It must have been a frightening blow to my grandparents when their only daughter among five sons was struck down suddenly with what was then called 'infantile paralysis'. Dark and bonny, at three years old, Kit must have already had the wide, generous cheekbones, candid eyes and slightly retroussée nose that I was to come to know so well. My grandfather told me of how Kit danced on the dining table the night before it happened – though I was always mystified at this part of the story for I could never imagine my grandmother allowing anybody to dance upon her dining table.

Next day Kit was almost totally paralysed after a restless, fever-ridden night. Two years of hospitalization and a long, uphill fight brought some measure of recovery. But it was limited alas, hence the calipers, the full length iron supports for her left leg topped with a round, leather bound ring, and the smaller not-so-necessary one for the right limb. So useful, of course, but such a pity all the same. It so happened that this disaster to Kit was only one of a series of hard knocks that came to Grandmother on whom eventually the burden of family troubles came to rest. As a pretty village girl – the 'village rose' she was, my Grandfather assured me – she had rejected a suitor who had some disability in favour of Grandfather who was lively, good-looking and a member of a well-connected Malvern family, though his tendency to jesting often seemed to offend her sense of the fitness of things in later life.

Within a year of their marriage Grandfather had been struck down with rheumatic fever. He never walked again without a pronounced limp and a physical weakness which impaired his ability to provide adequately for the children who came along as the years went by.

After his illness Grandfather became a 'snob', for he was obliged to find a new occupation at which he could be seated all day. In the little shop in Friar Street, behind and above which the family lived, he hammered away at other people's footgear in reasonable contentment. As customers came and went, in the easier pace of those years he was always ready for a lively chat, or to study and discuss 'form' in his affable way. Grandmother, hurrying through the shop on her brisk way to supplement the family income in some way or another (she was no 'clinging vine'), would bestow many a frown upon the friendly old cronies relaxing against the wooden counter and apparently  diverting Grandfather from the mound of boots and shoes, the stacks of hard, smelling leather around him and the neat piles of Cherry Blossom boot polish in various shades, of which 'Tonette' was always the best seller.

Beyond the communicating door we lived and ate in the warm, dim living room. Here, before the blackleaded range, Grandfather would relax in the evenings in his rounded wooden chair and light up his pipe from the curling tongues of flame, first pressing his spill against my red hair and professing mild astonishment when it did not crackle into flame.

In the evenings, in this living room two floors below her bedroom, Kit discarded the calipers, for they were cumbersome and prevented her relaxing her limbs at the fireside to enjoy the dancing tongues of flame that licked the bars of Grandmother's blackleaded grate. When it was time for bed Kit had no need to reharness the iron supports for she could slip her lifeless left leg across to her right knee and mount the two stairways in an adroit fashion, seated. Such a simple solution to what threatened in my imagination to be an insoluble struggle, quite astonished me the first time I accompanied her progress up what Grandfather unfailingly referred to as 'the wooden hill'.

Within a few days of my coming to stay with Kit (it was a month before her eighteenth birthday), we fell into a bedtime routine by which I preceded her up the dark staircases – and I have to confess to being impatiently clumsy at times – with the flickering candlestick in one hand and a half cup of cocoa in the other, shedding a little from each on the way. This obviously left a great deal to be desired in a cup-bearer, but since the cocoa was provided to sustain Kit in the night when she awoke, dry and rasping, she had a vested interest, so to speak, and made no protest beyond the occasional dismayed gasp upon the stairs.

If truth be told, Kit was inclined to gurgle slightly when imbibing the cocoa in moments of waking stress, a sound which, as most of humanity will know, is inclined to put a strain on the affections and to produce an antipathy toward cocoa dregs, if one is in close proximity. Nevertheless, this was a small price to pay for Kit's warm company in the dark hours, to share her not inconsiderable library and to browse over her overflowing scrapbook which was private and personal to us who occupied this bedroom.

So, in that wakeful Midnight Hour early in 1924, my thoughts turned to the scrapbook. Last night we had pored over the loose cuttings by the indifferent light of that same candle, indulging our griefs and dreams in turn. Most impressed was I by the little verse penned, I believe, by some Methodist parson. His name escapes me, but his words live on:

Love has a hem to its garment that reaches the very dust.
It can touch the stains
Of the streets and lanes –
And, because it can, it must.

Good deeds took shape like a crusader's cross in the flickering shadows on Kit's bedroom wall, and it did not cross my mind for a moment that the peevish slopping of Kit's cocoa on the stairs, in the half formed hope that it would discourage the nightly indulgence she enjoyed, did anything to violate the lofty aspirations which were taking shape in my mind.

I yawned and realized I was getting drowsy again. 'Oh

well, might as well settle,' I thought, until I was struck
by a new problem. Had I said my prayers before I fell
asleep earlier? I couldn't remember clearly - well, yes, I
could remember starting them with the familiar phrase
which I found a bit off-putting though I couldn't very well
tell anybody so: 'Gentle Jesus, meek and mild...' but
could recall no more. I must have dropped off in the
middle. So should I start again? I supposed I must. After
all, God cannot be expected to remember where you left
off the first time...

'Look upon a little child...' The words were
mechanically framing themselves in my mind when a nasty
thought shot through me. Kit might have said just that,
fifteen years ago, when she went to sleep fit and well and
then woke up next day and couldn't move properly, not
her arms, nor her legs, nor even her neck. It was
fearsome, what could happen to people. I stretched my
legs down the bed, despite the colder climate of the lower
half, and wriggled my toes. Yes, they all worked quite
well and I was tempted to draw them back up into the
warmer area again. But I wouldn't grow so well if I did -
and I was rather tired of being called 'Titch' at school. I
ate all my crusts up, like folks told me, but I didn't get
much bigger. Perhaps that was because crusts were no
sacrifice to me - I liked them better than soft bread. So
maybe it didn't work for me.

Kit had become aware of my leg movements down the
bed - 'Feet cold, Pet?' she asked solicitously, and without
waiting for reply she somehow manoeuvred the stone hot
water bottle towards me with her stronger right foot. It
was comforting, and by its aid I found it much, much
easier to stretch and grow and I resumed my prayers with
more enthusiasm, for now I had got to the stage where I
could, in all conscience, add my own requests.

I wanted Mother and the new baby to get well, of
course, and come back home again, but I would like to
stay in Friar Street, for somehow in that strange and
wakeful hour I had sensed the first, faint stirring of pride
and awe in Worcester's historic associations. It was a
factor which ultimately would add life and colour to my
small span. And probably all because those Cathedral
chimes summoned me in the still of the night from across
the few intervening roof tops, to think of those who slept
on, way below the belfry, hearing no sound.

I thought of the gentle boy, Prince Arthur, wrapped in

his 'most lovely little house' as Arthur Mee called it, though to me it was like a fairytale palace made of icing sugar. How sad for him, and even more so for the little Spanish princess, Catherine of Aragon, who was his widow. He was still only fifteen years old when he died, and their marriage but a few weeks back. He never had the chance to show whether he had the kingly qualities of his stern Tudor father. Maybe not ... and perhaps not all the sober prayers of his Spanish princess could have sustained him in that difficult role.

But surely - oh, surely - he would have made a better job of it than the infamous King John who lay so near to him in the central aisle before the High Altar. Only a few days earlier I had learned at school the tale of John's deeds and misdeeds, of his Isabelle and Isabella (what a coincidence) and about The Barons, Magna Carta, Runnymede and The Wash. The story had progressed to the stage where the King lost all his jewels in The Wash and I, who had never held a real jewel in all my eight years of life, thought this the ultimate, as well as the most unnecessary, of all his woes. It vexed me to think that this careless mishap had no silver lining for a living soul, then or since so far as I could judge, for *nobody,* Miss Barker had impressively assured us, had ever found the treasure again. Stubbornly I was, even then, groping for a world in which every calamity had some compensating merit.

But now he lay, only a few hundred yards away, in the safe sanctity of our Cathedral. I felt immensely consoled that at the end of his troubled life, though the rest of his family and even Isabella, lay in some old abbey in Western France, he had asked to be brought to this, his favourite city, to lie between St Wulstan and St Oswald. Legend had it that he was clad at the last in the simple brown habit of a monk. I wondered curiously if God was impressed by his belated piety, as indeed I was. Even then I had a weakness for prodigals, and for strong men brought low.

It was all his own fault, I supposed, that he came to such a sorry end and lost our empire and all that. It felt better if you realized that it was his own fault. It balanced things up somehow and made more sense of life. Those tight little corners around Grandmother's small mouth... Maybe it was because of her rejection of that unfortunate suitor with the limp that her burdens came.

But it was rough on Kit... In fact it was very rough on Kit.

CHAPTER 2

The Apollo

AS IF IT WERE NOT BLISS enough to be christened by the exotic name of Olga, the child next door to my grandparents' at Number Twenty Five Friar Street had the good fortune to be born in a sweet shop – or above it, which is just as good if your father owns it. And it was quite the best in the locality.

True Sigley's, just up the road, boasted its own factory in which to produce Mother Sigley's Cough Sweets from a secret recipe. They were sold from big glass jars on the counter and shot into little triangular bags bearing the printed likeness of Mother Sigley, mittened hands in lap. Having sampled her wares (Uncle Sidney championed them) I found it hard to believe such a demure old soul could concoct anything so vile as those lozenges – the word 'sweets' was a misnomer.

Fancy wrappings and secret recipes notwithstanding, Evans's sweet shop was the one that brought a new dimension into our lives, Naomi's and mine.

Olga was a bonny child, her hair sleek and black with an uncompromising fringe surmounting friendly grey eyes which first met mine when I climbed upon a dustbin at the foot of Grandfather's premises and peeped curiously over the high dividing wall into her rear garden. And it truly was a garden, not a blue brick yard like those which served most of the shop premises adjoining it.

Olga was the youngest member of the Evans household, which included two very grown up brothers who were already well established as hairdressers (quite distinct from the amazing number of barbers around us), an elder sister whose nose wrinkled in the most engaging manner when she laughed, which was quite often, and two bachelor uncles who also followed the family flair for offering to the Worcester public commodities and services which could not long be resisted. They were pioneers after a fashion.

Mrs Evans, in addition to managing this large

household, ran the sweetshop. It was light, airy, well stocked and the goods attractively displayed. This was no mere booth dispensing ready wrapped wares with clinical precision - but a wonderland of jars, bottles, bins and serving shovels where the goods tickled your fancy even before reaching your palate.

Olga's mother never seemed to mind how long you took to make up your mind about the relative attractions of Jap Nuggets, Toasted Teacakes, Jelly Babies or Cadbury's halfpenny bars (which almost always won with me). She leaned cheerfully over the counter, her bright eyes dancing from you to the shelves and bottles while she made suggestions. When she ladled out the ice cream, made on the premises, from the big circular container behind the counter, she plumped it squarely into the crisp cornet with such goodwill as to stimulate anticipation and heighten the pleasure of the first lick.

Even after she had served you, she never hurried you away, but lingered near the counter with her dancing smile and really seemed to want to know about the new baby and our mother's health. Often Naomi and I were welcomed into the large, warm room behind the shop and out into the long garden beyond, where Olga's swing held pride of place beneath the branches of a sturdy oak. This walled garden was like an oasis in the desert of concrete, tarmac, cobblestones, brick and plate glass which made up the Friar Street business world.

Olga shared swing and family with equal generosity. Only once we climbed the dim, twisting staircase and saw her father, for he appeared to be a constant invalid. His two bachelor brothers were much more part of the scene.

Uncle Frank rode a tricycle converted to an ice cream dispenser, pedalling his way through the old streets to the riverside where he found lots of customers among the trippers inveigled here by our stretch of the Severn. Between customers, he rested upon his handlebars to chat to all who had leisure to sit upon the benches and feed the swans.

Uncle Bert Evans owned a large black saloon car - the first person of our acquaintance to do so. It doubled as a taxi when clients were available and for family expeditions on other occasions. When I first caught sight of him behind the wheel in the cab rank outside Shrub Hill station, I thought him very impressive with his peaked cap and dapper moustache, and not unlike the pictures of Ronald Colman who was all the rage at that time.

It was due to Uncle Bert that I carried away that year's prize for the best wild flower collection, for nature study would never have been my forte if I had been obliged to rely upon my own two feet. We made it a family affair, tracking down different species, drying and pressing them between the pages of a heavy book and presenting them neatly fixed and labelled by an appointed date. With Uncle Bert at the wheel I progressed beyond buttercups and daisies to such delights as cowslips, campion, kingcup, ragwort, violets, anemones, ladysmock, sorrel, water lilies and even the occasional wild orchid in the lanes and meadows of Worcestershire. I can taste the pleasure of discovery still!

I am not sure which of the three Evans brothers it was who developed the additional (and crowning) enterprise. Maybe it was a combined operation which enabled them to break away from their other demanding roles on Saturdays and run the back street cinema known officially as The Apollo in Park Street, and more familiarly dubbed The Fleapit. And all for the benefit of the children of the neighbourhood.

Hitherto the world of cinemas and theatres had been taboo to my family by virtue of our tender years and my father's predilection for the Gospel Hall just around the corner from his shop, in Charles Street. This was our first Sunday School and very much a part of our family scene, but while our mother was away, our normal routine was suspended.

We were intrigued by the busy preparations at the Evans's for their Saturday rendezvous. Possibly the cinema having been out of bounds hitherto added to its charm, but now Grandmother saw no harm in accepting the neighbourly invitation for Naomi and me to join Olga, and I took refuge from my uneasy conscience by virtue of our going there not as ordinary patrons but by courtesy of the management.

Thither we were borne one Saturday afternoon by Olga's Uncle Frank in Uncle Bert's taxi, loaded with equipment. If our arrival passed unnoticed, it was only because we came an hour before the impatient, noisy queue began to form on the pavement.

Just before three o'clock the big double doors of 'The Apollo' swung ajar to admit the boisterous patrons. They elbowed their way up to the Box Office where some member of the Evans family was in attendance, then dashed off to The Pit or Gallery according to the price paid for admittance. It was said that those unable to muster cash could gain entry on production of jam jars, but this awkward form of currency never found its way back with us in the returning taxi.

The best vantage point was the front row of the gallery facing the screen, and here Olga's party sat in the equivalent of the Royal Box, savouring a delicious mixture of anticipation and importance.

The projection room was way behind us as we sat in the gallery, and Olga's elder sister Edna preferred to take her place with the operator in the small metal compartment which had somehow been attached to the outside wall of the building to minimise fire risk. We rather envied her

this distinction but she took it as of right, for she had
been born in this building when the family, then
caretakers, lived in the basement flat below. Since she was
born in a palace (albeit a picture one) and nobody else in
Worcester had a like pedigree, she claimed a degree of
royalty and this, with her extra few years, gave her
precedence over us. Occasionally she was allowed to
operate the projector and since this was done manually, by
means of a winding movement, the projection speed was apt
to fluctuate with the operator's emotions. This was
particularly apparent with Edna at the controls. In
moments of excitement the picture sped by at incredible
speed, but during the tender, affecting moments of pathos
or romance Edna's arm definitely slowed as she followed
the story with the same rapt attention as we did. When
her arm practically ceased its motions while she savoured
the depth of the heroine's predicament or hung upon her
wide-eyed gaze fringed with beautiful dark eyelashes,
Edna would be brought back to earth and movement by the
stampede of feet from below and the rising crescendo of
catcalls from inferior creatures who were less blessed with
sympathetic faculties.

Despite the turmoil, at The Apollo we became well
acquainted with the cartoon characters of the day. Felix
the Cat was making his debut, his frequent appearances
on the screen being greeted with noisy affection and
hearty renderings of the theme song:

> *Fee-ee-lix kept on walking, kept on walking still,*
> *With his hands behind him, you will always*
> > *find him...*

The music was drowned by the noisy carollers and time
was beaten remorselessly by one hundred pairs of feet
upon the wooden floor.

But the pièce de résistance was the serialized version
of an Edgar Wallace thriller called 'The Green Archer'. It
was a silent film and unfortunately we did not stay with
Grandmother long enough to see the final instalment.
However, thrills were many as we followed with rapt
attention the progress of the masked archer, who shot his
way (by bow and arrow of course) out of his own
predicaments and those of other innocents, with perfect
timing. Each instalment ended abruptly with a crescendo of
sound followed by the flashing across the screen of a swift

injunction: 'TO BE CONTINUED! Don't miss next week's thrilling climax! How will the Green Archer...? etc., etc.' At this point I would draw a long breath, look back along the shaft of dusty light to the projectionist's box and feel immensely reassured that the Evans family was in control all the time!

It was only a matter of seconds before the audience regained their equilibrium and vocal powers, clattering and shrieking their way to the exits with realistic and spontaneous performances of this scene or that. Each departing client was regaled with an apple, an orange or a 'comic' to sustain his goodwill until the following Saturday. Eventually we too wended our way outside, closing the doors upon the dusty, mud-scraped seats and littered floor, banishing from mind the boos, catcalls, cheers and tears which had accompanied this afternoon's entertainment.

Up in Kit's room at night I mused dreamily over the events of the day, mentally projecting myself into the adventures and crises, meeting both with dogged courage in the manner of the heroine of the day. Perhaps it was not for nothing that somebody had yelled 'Ginger for pluck!' when my hair was pulled violently on the way out. Finally, tomboy though I was, or meant to be, I would permit myself the secret luxury of lingering over the more tender scenes with their inevitable happy climax at the altar. Even so, it did not cross my mind for a fleeting second that I really would stand one day as a bride in The Apollo. Perhaps truth *is* stranger than fiction...

* * * * *

So the weeks sped by until our Mother's return from Essex with the tiny, frail baby Muriel Olive. It was found now that she had her hands too full to resume care of Naomi, me, three-year-old Ernest *and* the hardware shop in Lowesmoor which was our secondary business as well as our home. Added to this was the effect of the economic depression upon our whole country, so it was not surprising that a family conclave resulted in a decision to bring all of our troubles under one roof. We sold off the vinegar, paraffin and soap in job lots and transported the more suitable of the stock to Father's 'real' shop in Friar Street, only about a hundred yards north of our Grandfather's shoe repair business.

The toys and fancy goods did not look at all out of place in the one half of the double-fronted building, whilst the opposite window gave precedence to the furnishings, pictures and household items which made up our main lines. True the accommodation over the shop was not designed for a growing family and left much to be desired domestically, but I personally felt no sense of deprivation. The stock of toys and fancy goods made us the envy of our more affluent cousins and the loss of a garden was offset by our father taking us often to The Promenade, the lawned area between the Cathedral and the river, bounded by a grey stone wall for safety. Here we could run and play and admire our father's prowess with a ball, for he was an excellent 'spinner' and had been captain of both cricket and football teams in his single days.

So here in Friar Street we were at the hub of everything - sights, smells, sensations, the lot. And there were plenty! Our immediate vicinity boasted a butchery, a bakery, a fried fish shop, a large pub, a corn and seed merchant's granary, and an anglers' store complete with wriggling livestock, so one might truly claim 'all human life was there' and a bit more too.

It may not be your idea of felicity to live directly opposite to a 'pub', but it does add colour to your scene. The clientele of the Eagle Vaults was drawn largely from the tenements and courtyards in our area. Many of them worked, if at all, in nearby factories and had families bigger than their incomes. With so many little 'uns occupying limited space at home, it is not surprising that many adults sought temporary refuge in the pub.

The landlord, at the time we arrived on the scene, was rather a 'gent', unfitted for the rigours of his trade. But he had the foresight to marry a woman ideally suited to it. She it was who, at closing times, flung out the reprobates, her abounding energy and 'Brummie' accent both contributing to her success, as three small faces pressed to an upstairs window opposite to the pub could testify. Before her irate figure Paddy Flynn went sprawling into the gutter frequently. Arms akimbo she would express her opinion of him in no uncertain terms before turning with a flourish to re-enter the door over which her husband stood guard. Reaching the threshold before our fascinated gaze she looked back at the recumbent Paddy and the group standing around in sympathetic stupor, and gave one final thrust which became the punch line in the family amateur dramatics which the scene inspired: 'If you wuz my 'usband I'd drahn yuh, that's what I'd do!'

Only slightly more respectable was the dramatic scene inspired by the confectionery bags issued with Ben Embling's wares in the nearby Shambles. Here a lusty, wailing lad was shown thrust face down upon his parent's knee, being belaboured by an energetic palm while the victim was bidden: 'Take that! And that! And the next time I send you for sweets, go to Embling's!'

Alas, the economic depression was creeping relentlessly over England and though family businesses around us were fairly safe since their customers were consumers in the literal sense, ours was more of a luxury trade – especially the new furnishings and toys – which felt the pinch first. My father adapted his business to a part exchange mart. Secondhand goods became the main stock in trade, yielding an interesting area of bric-a-brac and our wares became much more individual. Outside our shop window Father placed a few articles to attract passers by, using to full advantage the corner provided by the forward-jutting wall of our neighbour, Ye Olde Citie Bakerie. Around each article thus displayed he drew a half circle in white chalk to discourage passing dogs from confusing chair legs with the trees from which they sprang. Now and again we were ticked off by a passing bobby for obstructing the pavement. I lurked out of sight inside the shop, but Father was ever one for diplomacy. He would cheerfully, though quite temporarily, rectify the situation.

Mother was fussy about dusting and polishing stock now she was on the premises, but Father held to the theory that better trade was done when the place looked a little shabby. Tourists who thronged our ancient street would hover more hopefully around a shop which looked as if in charge of a feeble soul who might not be alert to the value of his wares.

Picture framing now became a useful standby. Photographs in those days were not hidden away in albums or projected on screens. They lined the walls of postwar parlours and bedrooms or adorned the mantlepiece – a 'must' in every self-respecting home, however short the money coming in. Soldier sons and husbands thus continued to gaze steadily upon the families they fought to defend but to whom they never returned. Some customers became testy when their framed treasures were not ready for them on the anticipated date, and could not seem to grasp that it was only Father's incurable optimism, or desire to please, which had precipitated him into promising the job much earlier than he could possibly accomplish it. My earliest apprenticeship into business consisted of being the one to answer the bellring of such customers, it being possible for Father to spy from the stairwell just who came in and to assess their likely requirements. It was as well that I held to my personal conviction that Father was doing his best.

Sometimes I perched upon a bench in the basement below the shop and watched my father at work on these important commissions. First placing the big T-shaped rule over a large sheet of clear glass, he would then, with pursed lips and a decisive stroke, skim the diamond cutter across the face of it producing a sharp, mounting screech until it reached the required length and depth. The rule was then laid aside. He lifted the diamond-scored sheet of glass and snapped it apart along the cut edges to form the required shape and size. Just occasionally he failed to achieve a clean break, and with only the barest tightening of lips and brows he would toss aside the mis-shapen effort and start afresh.

Stacks of moulding in gilt, oak, mahogany and what-have-you lined the basement walls and filled overhead racks ready for customers' selection, later to be sawn to the required size, neatly mitred at the corners, fitted together with a generous dab of the rich brown glue bubbling merrily away in the little iron cauldron on the nearby gas ring, and finally secured with a tiny brass pin tapped obliquely and invisibly across each corner.

After this I watched fascinated as the frame was turned face down on the bench to receive the cut sheet of glass which miraculously fell into place. Out came the yellow duster which had been hanging at half mast from Father's trouser pocket and dust and smears were banished from the inner surface of the glass. The customer's picture was then laid face down upon it, bedded down with matchwood, sealed over the back with strong brown paper and fitted with two hanging screws and a tiny red label to say where it had all been done.

I would sigh with satisfaction. It was a tremendous accomplishment, and I knew next time the customer came to the shop in hopeful anticipation (or near despair) the finished product would give such pleasure that the waiting time would be all forgotten.

No 3 Friar Street

CHAPTER 3

The Hardwicke Line

IT IS DOUBTFUL whether Friar Street held the same fascination for our mother as for me. No kitchen sink drama could touch the dregs quite so realistically as her attempts to cater for a family without a kitchen.

To begin with, our one and only brass tap was domiciled eighteen inches above floor level at the back of the shop below stairs! There must have been times when our mother fervently regretted Father surrendering his 'safe' job in the County Health Department to enter private enterprise, but somehow she coped in such a way that we were not really aware of being impoverished. I even had the impression (Heaven knows from where) that we were a 'cut above' the children of the district whose fathers went to work in cloth cap and muffler at the nearby tin factory which was the Metal Box Company in embryo, or made their way through the back streets to the vinegar works to produce Worcester Sauce.

The truth was our parents had a very real love for each other, so the atmosphere generally betrayed very little of the stress which must have been their experience. Father was an incurable optimist, which is of benefit to any family, but it was our mother's mingled practicality and sense of humour which carried us over many a hurdle.

She was one of the Worcestershire Hardwickes, some of whom have a gift for mimicry, a taste for the apt phrase and a love of drama. The most notable of them in the nineteen-twenties was Sir Cedric Hardwicke, the great character actor. It was a great day for me when the local schoolchildren were marshalled in crocodile to a local cinema to see his performance in the title role of 'Nelson'. And the Hardwickes had older claims to fame.

'Do you know, Kathie,' Aunt Gertrude assured me impressively, 'The Hardwickes are descended from King Canute!'

I was startled. 'Are you sure, Auntie?', I asked, incredulous at first. 'Can you tell, after so long?'

'Oh, yes,' she responded, with an assurance that brooked no argument, in what I recognized to be true Hardwickian style. 'Cousin Ernest has traced the family tree. Our line comes through his son, King Hardicanute.'

Cousin Ernest, the local school 'boardman', could be relied upon as a serious source of information, being employed by the educational authorities and entrusted by them to ascertain daily whether absentee schoolchildren were skiving or not. To dive back into the past and find out what Hardicanute had been up to would not be beyond him and his little leather-bound book in which he wrote down all the particulars entrusted to him in our day.

You may argue that a number of history books report that 'Hardicanute died without issue,' but this merely goes to show how unreliable even textbooks may be and, should any sceptic with shorter pedigree question the slight

discrepancy in the spelling of the family name, may I
humbly point out that even the Great Dane himself was
referred to in earlier writings as 'Cnut'. They were not
particular about individual letters in those days and
spelling is nothing whatever to go by.

The more I considered it, the more convincing it was.
Who but a drama-conscious Hardwicke would choose to
repudiate the flattery of his courtiers by sitting in a pool
of water? Had he been a mere Smith, Brown or Robinson
he would have bidden those conniving cronies to 'get
stuffed' when they predicted that the waves would roll
back for him, and our history books would have been so
much the duller.

Our shop being so near the city centre, The Shambles,
Woolworth's and all such necessary amenities, we saw more
of our relations than hitherto, for they could call for the
odd cup of tea whilst resting from their shopping sprees.
This was a welcome diversion for me, but I doubt whether
any of our Worcester folks gave me more food for thought
than Aunt Gertrude or demonstrated more clearly by their
own personalities that they were no nonentities. I couldn't
wait until she came again with further information. I made
my way to the Public Library. There might be some clue
as to whether Hardicanute had ever been in our city.

There was. I have to admit to being a bit abashed at
first to discover that Hardicanute's main claim to notoriety
in Worcester seems to be that he burned the city to the
ground in 1041. On behalf of the family, at this late
stage, I can only offer my apologies and plead mitigating
circumstances.

It appears that the citizens of that day took umbrage at
the heavy taxation levied against all Britishers and them in
particular, and decided that actions spoke louder than
Notices of Appeal to the Assessment Committee. They met
and chased from the City gate in Sidbury the two official
tax-gatherers (they were earls, no less), cornered them
beneath the Edgar Tower whence they fled for refuge en
route for the Cathedral sanctuary, and proceeded to stop
their little gallop with the Danegeld by hacking them to
pieces and afterwards wallpapering the outer door of this
entry to the Cathedral with portions of their skin.

In later years I too came to find that the lodging of tax
appeals against officials who are their own judge and jury
is a tiresome business. But - taken as an alternative -
this Night of the Long Knives was going a bit far.

Hardicanute thought so, at any rate. He despatched his
legions to pillage this City of Spires and burn it to the
ground. The citizens (there could not have been a vast
number) fled to an island off the banks of the Severn at
the spot we call Bevere and here camped until the fires
glowed less ruddily. They then returned, possibly
reflecting that you can't win against the Inland Revenue,
and set about rebuilding this noble city.

You may well wonder how the Hardic-Canutes found
time to perpetuate their dynasty in Worcester with so much
going on, but of their virility there can be little doubt,
whatever the textbooks say. Here and there family touches
come to light in the manors and villages which bear their
name. On one document concerning the transfer of a
property in the county, no less a signatory than
Hardicanute's own mother has left her mark. Queen Emma
is a distinguished forbear in her own right, for she was
wife to two Kings of England (she married her husband's
conqueror) and mother to two others. She came from the
Court of Normandy and made her conquests more than fifty
years before her great-nephew William set foot upon our
shores and established his. In point of fact, had it not
been for Emma's role in England's history, we would never
have had that remarkable line of Norman and Plantagenet
rulers in this country.

So, with all due respect to my Aunt Gertrude, my own
researches favour the redoubtable Emma, mother of
Hardicanute, as the real figure of destiny in our family
tree. True she was not awfully popular, and had a habit
of falling out with her relations, but you can't please all
the people all the time.

True to her heritage and to her family's dramatic
talents, Mother found time to regale us with many a tale of
her own family life. Theirs was one of the larger branches
of the Hardwicke tree, and those whom we never met came
alive in our imagination and we valued every one of them.
Alas, not many of that colourful family made old bones
but, deprived of their acquaintance in the flesh, we
listened the more intently to what Mother told us of them,
if only because of the delightful way in which she did so.
Despite her predilection for beauty (disconcerting to a
child who had not inherited that advantage), she was not
averse to using a wry expression or a telling grimace when
her tale so demanded.

To us her eldest brother could never have been more

than a handsome face beneath a soldier's peaked cap, or
the slim young violinist with the shock of beautiful hair
who gazed gravely up at us from the surface of well
thumbed postcards, had he not come to life in Mother's
revelations, for he was one of The Fallen. But in their
earlier family life, he was the eldest brother and their
mother's mainstay and champion, prudent and
hardworking. He maintained his pedal bike in spotless
condition, strung up to the roof of an outhouse when not
in use, so that not even the tyres touched the ground. It
was a treasure which had not been acquired without
stringent economies. But a younger brother would sneak it
out on occasions and try to return it undetected.
Inevitably the day came when bike and brother together
came to grief at the foot of a hill.

Summoned to the scene, their mother ran down, stared
aghast at her bleeding, breathless offspring lying prone
on the cobbles and stood transfixed with the words 'Poor
Will! Poor Will!' escaping from ashen lips. Which might not
have been surprising except that it was Jim who lay on
terra firma, his sins revealed for all to see. Will was the
owner of the bike, at that moment pursuing his normal
course, in blissful though temporary ignorance of his
mother's anguished concern for him.

We made only briefly the acquaintance of our
Grandfather Hardwick, irreverently called Fat Grand-dad,
only in contrast to our other (Lawrence) one. He was a
controversial character it transpired, self-educated to a
remarkable degree but condemned by circumstances to
factory labour. Deep-thinking but inhibited, he attempted
to drown his sorrows in the nearest 'local', only to find
this had the effect of producing more. Destruction and
disruption flared up in the home on his return therefrom,
with results which would have provided a telling case
history for the then active Band of Hope, had they known
it.

It was what this did to their longsuffering, loving
mother that drove the elder sons to issue an ultimatum
when they came of age. Either he left, or they did. In one
of his more lucid moments, Grand-dad Hardwick must have
recognized that his earnings were on the wane, whereas
theirs were sorely needed and conscientiously shared in a
family where so many were still at school.

Whether it was the recollection of the day when he
departed that brought the wounded look into my mother's

face when she recounted it, or of the day when he
returned on a visit more than a year later I cannot recall.
He came dressed in his Sunday suit, Mother said, and sat
awkwardly on a tall chair in their kitchen-cum-living room,
his bowler hat upon his knees, and came to terms.

There is something about the sight of a strong man
humbled which diminishes most of us, and I wished my
Grandmother Hardwick had lived long enough for me to see
her just once to show my support for her welcome-back
gesture, even if it had to be vetted by her faithful
troops. I dare to say there has been many an unsung act
of feminine diplomacy in like humble surroundings which
far outshines the logic of the generals who come to a
loftier truce table. For me the telling of this tale amply
justified my mother's lifelong detestation of strong drink.
It was not only for the peace of the family, but for the
sake of her father's own dignity.

The family had their lighter moments, of course. They
were able to smile at the recollection of the neighbour's
children who, in late evening, camped out on their
doorstep and confided, apparently without surprise or
rancour:

> *Our Dad's come 'ome drunk an' we've all got*
> *t'ave a good 'idin'. Our Floss and our Bill's*
> *'ad theirs, but me an' our Joe ain't 'ad ours*
> *yet.*

The logic of this drunken father puzzled and fascinated
me in turn. Could it be that he needed the added strength
of his liquor to catch up with his family's past
misdemeanours - or were the hidings given in advance in
anticipation of sins yet to be committed? Either way it felt
much the same, I presumed, and I never failed to admire
the admirable resignation with which it was accepted. I
scarcely know what a psychologist would make of this, but
it could be that such an upbringing provided a far better
preparation for the indiscriminate blows of Fate than falls
to the lot of children more thoughtfully nurtured. Some of
us stagger still in fruitless rejection of the way in which
the best laid plans of mice and men turn out.

On the marvellous days when the postman brought a
large, impressively stamped brown paper parcel which had
travelled all the way from Montreal, we not only enjoyed
the luscious chocolates all of two inches in diameter, but

loved to recall that these came from our Auntie Nell, mother's eldest sister who, with nothing more than a servant's wages, had contrived a passage to Canada. A pioneer indeed, I thought, having enjoyed a spate of tales about those who had sown the seeds of our Empire. It has to be confessed, however, that empire building was not Auntie Nell's main objective. She had made the unfortunate discovery whilst 'living in' as a maid-of-all-work, that she was to have a child - whilst the father, unaware of his prowess, had gone off to Canada. Not for Auntie Nell the weeping, wailing and admonition of employer and family alike. Having already been forced of necessity to 'put her feet under somebody else's table' and so relieve her family's overcrowding, she had achieved a sturdy independence by the time she was eighteen years old. She mustered her slender resources, bought a one-way ticket for Canada and was on the high seas before anybody knew of her predicament. This was in true Hardwickian style I thought, but more was to follow.

She could not have been entirely certain of the reception of her news on the other side of the Atlantic, and after a few days on the ocean wave she came to terms with life as it was. She remembered that a bird in hand was worth two in the bush, and accepted the proposal of marriage from a fellow passenger who had had the sense to recognize her sterling worth and fall in love with her. He made a wonderful father for her daughter Gladys and loved Auntie Nell devotedly for the rest of his life, though no more offspring ever came.

So Cousin Gladys was an 'only one'. A highly privileged state in my estimation, which judgement was reinforced on the occasion of the one and only visit of mother and daughter to our humble domicile in Friar Street. Auntie Nell was jolly and plump, just as I pictured her, though that picture was not so much a feat of the imagination as of the recollection that when six-year-old Gladys had entered school (they did not start at five years as the spartan English did) she had been unmercifully teased by some classmates. Her mother was puzzled at her reluctance to return to school next day to 'all the nice little friends you've made, Gladys honey', until Gladys threw her arms around Auntie Nell's neck and wailed: 'I don't care what they say about you - I *like* my little fat Mommie!'

Needless to say the recital of this dialogue in a letter sent to our mother did nothing to commend the manners of

Canadian schoolchildren, but presented a very agreeable picture of short, plump, cheerful Auntie Nell long before her visit to us. Looking then upon Gladys's frills, bonnets, curls and furbelows we concluded she had a lot going for her anyway, and were not at all surprised to hear a few years later that she had eloped from High School to marry a *crooner!* Not at that time being acquainted with the merits of crooners - they were new to our generation - we expressed some misplaced condolences with Auntie Nell, only to discover later that our transatlantic cousin had done quite well for herself. Dick Todd made a name for himself and the word crooner was eventually made quite respectable by one Bing Crosby.

So it occurs to me that the Hardwicks had a very reasonable philosophy. Auntie Nell may have inherited hers from our Fat Grand-dad. There was the day (apparently during a spell of domestic harmony) when the latter came home to a meatless meal and wrily acknowledged that at least he was no worse off than a toothless workmate who pitifully proclaimed in the works canteen earlier that day: 'Anybody can 'ave the "mate" if Oi can 'ave the suction.'

It seems to me in retrospect there must have been some meatless days for us in Friar Street of necessity, when 'suction' was all our mother could muster for her growing brood. Mercifully she was a marvel with stews... and with kids... and with customers, who always preferred her sympathetic attention in the shop if they could get it... and of course with our father too, for she never disguised that she loved him greatly.

So perhaps it was not surprising that we came home from school one day to find that unexpectedly (so far as I was concerned at any rate) we had been joined by a pert little soul with a crop of ginger down all over his scalp. They called him Edgar James, and cheerfully we all slid up one and made room for him.

* * * * *

Unfortunately our other small brother, Ernest, developed a wanderlust. This was discovered while we, together with one or two other aunts and cousins, were on a visit to our nice, plump Aunt Mabel in Birmingham. We found Aunt Mabel's house down an alleyway at the rear of a large, well-stocked boot and shoe store in Nechells. As with many industrial areas of those years, business premises dominated the street frontages, while the courtyards behind were occupied by small terraced dwellings approached via an entry beside the shops.

Here for a time we played outside with the children of the neighbouring house, three sisters named respectively Ena, Una and Ina. It troubled me a little, contemplating the trio, wondering what their parents would do for names if they doubled the number of their offspring and ran out of vowels. Our acquaintance was too short to settle this issue and presently I tired of their company, finding the grown-ups gossip much more to my liking. I remembered last Christmas when we had all congregated at the home of another aunt to celebrate the birth of the Prince of Peace. While the youngsters played blind man's buff in the parlour, our mothers were having a furious row in the kitchen. It took three attempts on their part to dislodge me from the kitchen door before I could reconcile myself to returning and making the best of blind man's buff.

Here in Nechells the atmosphere was very cordial, but I was disappointed; because his speech was so different from our own, Uncle Billy contributed little to the conversation. In between tea, buns and sandwiches Aunt Mabel regaled us with the story of how the shoe shop proprietor in the front premises had won through to success against all odds.

'They came with nothing but what they stood up in,' she assured us impressively. 'Every halfpenny they possessed went into stock. As for furniture, they sat on packing cases and fed off wooden crates. And now look at them!'

We did, and as a mark of our goodwill Mother bought Naomi and me some sandals. Wondering if our small brother would feel affronted unless treated likewise, she looked round for him. But four year old Ernest had vanished, apparently into thin air - if Nechells boasted any of that rarefied commodity. He was missing for more than two hours, while the hands of the clock on Aunt Mabel's mantlepiece were moving inexorably towards the time of our excursion's return. Finally it was Uncle Billy who found him, sitting on the bottom step of a public house a quarter of a mile away, being fed on crisps by the publican's wife.

Uncle Billy claimed great credit for this discovery, which he put down to his commonsense in questioning all the women neighbours and shoppers, then taking the opposite direction to that which they indicated. Thankful

for results, we all applauded him the first time he drew
attention to his strategy. Some even murmured approval
the second time round. After that his credit rating went a
bit low. Aunt Mabel came out with her suspicion that Uncle
Billy had merely been seeking to refresh himself during
the Great Search when he came across Ernest by chance.

FRIAR STREET, WORCESTER.

Friar Street – from the clockmenders to Eagle Vaults

CHAPTER 4

Where Friars Walked

I AM NO JUDGE of distances, but I should think about a hundred yards separated my father's shop from my grandfather's (numbered three and twenty-three respectively), and as by now sleeping accommodation in our improvised flat was at a premium, what better solution than for Naomi and me to rejoin Kit at nights. Now I was ten years old and it did not occur to me to object to the nightly trek. In my imagination we lived in a medieval castle. I simply skimmed from north wing to south to reach our boudoir, and all the intervening territory became especially mine.

I was forced to recognize that alien forces occupied part of our family thoroughfare, but the added interest of wares displayed well into late evening to either side of me as I progressed to bed, had something to be said for it.

Ye Olde Citie Bakerie always promoted a warm feeling, not alone for its savoury smells. Charlie Wall's family were homely, friendly and heartwarming people, though distinguished by owning the first petrol-driven delivery van in our locality. It was a real family enterprise in which Mrs Wall was busily occupied without losing her maternal warmth toward her own brood and extending it to ours.

Over to the right, on the opposite side of the road and adjoining Eagle Vaults, lived one known as Darkie Harding - presumably because of his natural colouring rather than his occupation of chimney sweep. But his black bowler hat also contributed to the colour scheme and I never saw him, frequently leaning against the doorpost of his little black and white cottage-cum-shop, without it. It seemed a little pretentious for one of his humble calling, yet reflection indicated that the bowler might prove the very thing for a man who battled daily beneath an avalanche of descending soot. My sister Naomi thought he was a spy, which was exciting though it was difficult to comprehend what secrets he could extract from other people's chimneys.

Alice Frost's big window at Number Twelve provided a lively contrast, for she could muster the most diverse assortment of secondhand clothing and accessories it is possible to take in with one pair of curious eyes. Her modern counterparts of 'Nearly New' and 'Beautiful Clothes' can never hold the candle to Alice for variety. Silver shoes, black-buttoned boots, arty crafty fans, woolly shawls, babies' bootees, tortoiseshell combs, snakecharm bracelets, bead necklaces, bangles and lockets took pride of place against a background of hanging garments. Flared skirts, pleats, frills and furbelows in an astonishing variety of colours, all of which might have seen better days, had not yet given up hope of a place in the sun and livened my nightly progress along Friar Street.

Ernie Watts' hardware display offered Monkey Brand

soap for those who wanted to see their faces mirrored in their frypans, and Pears' for those who were Preparing to be a Beautiful Lady. And what Pears' could not accomplish Ernie's sister Florence could, with her School of Dance whereby she transformed a score of oddly assorted schoolgirls into a delectable troupe of twinkling toe dancers. 'Let me have your two little girls,' she pleaded with my mother, 'the one so small and agile and the other so bonny and fair, I could do wonders with them! And it would be so good for them.' But the Gospel Hall around the corner, which was our Sunday rendezvous, did not approve of things theatrical so Naomi and I never had the chance to make the grade before the footlights, though I think it gave my mother some severe twinges of regret. Her high ideals conflicted with her weakness for pretty things and dainty feet.

And so, in no time at all, I arrived at the juncture along my nightly corridor where the upper storeys of Greyfriars and of Mr. Giles' clockmender's shop at Number Eighteen leaned across the road toward each other as if trying to exchange confidences. For all I know they may have been holding a consultation on the problem which engaged me every time I tripped past No 18. How on earth did Mr and Mrs Giles sleep soundly in a bedroom which had a visible slope downward from right to left over their shop window? Given the choice, I concluded, one would elect to sleep with one's head at the upper end of the gradient - but how did they prevent themselves from sliding to the foot of the bed in the dark hours and thus waking to find ankles protruding through separate brass rails? Now the building has been so beautifully restored, the outline of the black oak beam which runs across at bedroom floor level does nothing to resolve the mystery; if anything, it emphasizes the tilt.

Sometimes the stooped figure of Mr Giles could still be seen bending over a bench or counter as I passed in the evening, so it surprised me subsequently to discover that he sometimes failed to get his repairs done to time (no pun intended). His defence against impatient customers was undertaken by Mrs Giles at the shop counter, and argument with her availed very little, for the malady which rocked that lady's head unsteadily from side to side during the conversation, placed the customer at a disadvantage, to say the least. I never grasped the cause for Mrs Giles' condition and was forced to the conclusion that over-long association with other people's pendulums had done Mrs Giles no good – which made it all the more churlish of a customer to kick over the traces.

Greyfriars

But it was Greyfriars of course which held pride of place in our street and which gave it its famous name. The long black and white frontage had been split into four shops at ground floor level, three tiny ones to the left of the wide courtyard entrance, and a much larger one at the farther end. The first three comprised our much prized fish-and-chip shop, the home and workshop of a blind basket maker and the fruiterer's which housed the large and lively family of its proprietor overhead. It was the final and largest shop which held pride of place, not only because it was stacked throughout with secondhand books of all descriptions, but because of the strange figure who was both caretaker and shopkeeper. She was a gaunt spinster with long, black hair falling lankly over thin shoulders and way down her back. Her features were sallow, almost expressionless, cheekbones prominent beneath shadowed eyes.

Was it by chance Miss Wilmott came to Greyfriars, or had she been summoned there by voices which went unheeded by most of us? For Greyfriars was reputed to be haunted. And small wonder if it was, for the original occupants, grey-habited followers of St Francis, had been turned out by the avaricious King Henry VIII of ill-fame, who appeared to treat his subjects with as little respect as he treated his unfortunate wives. He sold it to Worcester Corporation for £540 and through the years it had deteriorated to near demolition stage. At some time the original Worcester prison had adjoined the Greyfriars site and the prison graveyard was said to lie at the rear, beyond the rough tenement dwellings that had been thrown up by some 19th century developer in the Greyfriars rear garden.

Miss Wilmott was reputed to be a spiritist medium and one could only hurry by the building in gathering dusk wondering if the voices which summoned her were those of the outraged, displaced and homeless monks or of the sadder creatures who had been numbered among the transgressors and silenced too soon by prison privations, or the hangman's noose, to make their peace with God or man. Either way it was not a comforting thought.

It was reported by neighbouring almshouse dwellers that in the night hours the spinster medium roamed the stairways and corridors of Greyfriars, candlestick aloft, chanting weird hymns or pronouncing chilling curses and - unholy of unholies - that the long white calico nightgown was often cast aside on these perambulations with results that were startling, to say the least, to any late night prowlers who let curiosity get the better of them.

By some curious stroke of fate, the medium was possessed of a son. It was not easy to fit this boy into the strange pattern of his mother's activities and I wondered how it fared with him in the wee, small hours. One could not help concluding, in later years, that his mother's vigils had not been always with the unquiet dead.

I marvelled as I pressed on toward Number Twenty Three, that so many barbers remained solvent in our street, but my Uncle Reg maintained that most of them had sidelines. 'Take old Plumper Baylis for instance,' he confided, 'He was a bookie on the side. One day a customer placed a bet with him for the 2.30 on Worcester Racecourse. The horse came in at 20 to 1 but Plumper had a bad day and could not pay out. He tried some delaying tactics.'

It appeared Plumper continued to have some bad days and eventually the irate customer, having repeated previous opinions concerning Plumper's integrity, brainpower and parentage, sat himself down in the barber's chair for a trim and shave in part payment of the debt. Unwisely he continued, labouring his point beyond Plumper's forbearance. Fortified by the tools of his trade, Plumper let out a roar: 'If you don't shut your trap – I'll cut your filthy throat!' Simultaneously he dipped his long steel razor into a bowl of boiling water and drew the back of it lightly but swiftly across his client's upturned throat.

With a yell that startled the neighbourhood, the victim sprang from the chair as if spring-loaded and fled the entire length of Friar Street, face plastered with lather, Plumper's towels flying behind him in the wind, yelling that he had been murdered!

I usually ran the rest of the way on my nightly beat because the tall iron railings of Laslett's Almshouses yielded little interest to one passing, apart from the reflection that behind them also was part of the gaol graveyard. But it was comforting to glance across to The Welcome Mission, that bulwark against the eeriness of Greyfriars, overindulgence at The Vaults, uncertainties of the turf, sharp practices and any other arrows of misfortune. Built by the Cadburys, it was overshadowed architecturally and socially by the Cathedral, but stood squarely and unequivocally with General Booth in his assertion:

Some like to dream within the sound of church
or chapel bell.
I'd rather run a rescue shop within a yard of Hell!

I believe the Cadburys themselves worshipped with the Quakers who (however they earned their name) had become known to us as a dignified and restrained community. But the Mission, through its white-haired Welsh-born Pastor Massey, proclaimed the plain man's gospel strongly tinged with teetotalism for it was also the rendezvous for the local Band of Hope. Lining the Mission walls were posters, the most potent of which (in my eyes) depicted a ragged, barefoot child beneath whom the brief caption 'MORE BEER - LESS BOOTS' spoke volumes. The later, somewhat derisory view of the Bands of Hope might be modified if that temperance movement were viewed against the backcloth of the times at the turn of the century. Certainly our bird's eye view of the undignified exits from the Eagle Vaults, and our slight acquaintance with some families of the neighbourhood, with their sad but regular patronage of the pawnshop down the road, justified the ballads and aspirations of the Band of Hope in my impressionable mind.

As a child I felt immensely proud of our local connection with the Cadburys, whose red and blue chocolate packs were known the world over. As the trade depression brought strikes, want and hunger, it was that family who came up, brisk and efficient, soup ladles at the ready, beneath the roof of Tudor House which, I believe, they then owned also.

If further evidence of practical religion were required, we got it on the best day out our local school ever afforded us - a visit to Bournville. I was impressed that the workers' amenities in this 'factory in a garden' were provided voluntarily by the employers. I then only dimly discerned that the preaching of total abstinence may be a negative doctrine - but I had no doubt whatever of the positive pleasure to be extracted from a bar of Cadburys Fruit and Nut!

* * * * *

On Saturday mornings it was not necessary to hurry up to No.3 for breakfast and to prepare for school, so I lingered with Kit and her books and magazines, or watched her clean the cutlery, which she did with unaccustomed patience. Quite often I would wander across the road and up the entry opposite to Grandfather's shop to find Stella Turberfield, with whom my first contact had come eighteen months before, during my earlier stay with my grandparents.

Stella was the eldest child of the Tudor House caretakers. Her mother looked after the big old building, polished the uneven oak floors and kept the surgeries and waiting rooms in a manner which befitted the school medical centre. Behind the building, and at the top of the entry alongside it, stood the caretaker's cottage. Here Stella and I played 'shop' with the contents of her mother's pantry, dressed our dolls, or ran about the courtyard, on more energetic pursuits which were often enlivened by Stella's brothers and their friends. It was a spacious place, paved with blue bricks, and proved an excellent spot for chalking hopscotch designs. But there were times when Stella was unexpectedly tired and disinclined for the livelier games which I favoured.

One day, a few weeks after the birth of our little brother, I discovered a pile of big wooden curtain rings amongst my father's stock and made my way across to Tudor House with the proposition of a hoop-la stall. I reached the cottage just as Mrs Turberfield was leaving it.

'Hallo,' she greeted me, but seemed a little abstracted, 'You can go on in and find Stella, but she's not well today. In fact, she is having to stay in bed. I'm sure she'd like to see you though. She's got a new book up there but she seems a bit too tired to look at it.'

I was shocked. Staying in bed on a *Saturday* morning was beyond thinking about. I hesitated but Mrs Turberfield turned back and I followed her into the large living room where 'Sonny' Turberfield was absorbed with his marbles, and the little sister was toddling around on some mission known only to herself and the one-eyed teddy she was dragging behind her by his right ear.

The staircase led off from one side of the living room and was enclosed by a door with a high latch. As Mrs

Turberfield raised this, her hands, coarsened by long years of heavy scrubbing and polishing, trembled slightly. I glanced at her curiously and noticed that the thin features looked tired and drawn. Some strands of hair had escaped the loose bun at the back of her head and strayed unchecked over her neck and shoulder. A slight feeling of apprehension touched me but within seconds we were in the sick room.

Stella was disinclined even for conversation that day. She lay very still against the white pillow and I became aware of a strange, yellow hue on her skin which seemed to have overtaken the customary freckles. We had sympathized with each other about the freckles, for we both suffered from them and had failed to fade them out even with the vinegar remedy recommended by one of Kit's magazines. Looking at her face now, it occurred to me that the freckles had not been so bad after all. Her hair, a darker auburn than mine, lay lank and lifeless each side of her face.

I made some effort to interest her in the new book, but though she rolled to one side, the better to face me, she had little to say. I was relieved when her mother returned and suggested I came again next day. 'I'll bring my new celluloid doll with me,' I offered, 'It's light as a feather. She could hold that in bed. Perhaps we could make some clothes for it...' Thankfully I escaped into the sunshine which filtered between the tall buildings, arriving home just as Mother was despatching a satisfied customer. To my annoyance I found the doll I sought had met with the weight of somebody's foot and come off worst, but Mother soothed my indignation by assurances of retribution and repair. Lighting the gas jet of her cooker, she held the dented body against the heat and by gentle propulsion and manipulation - hey presto, it came up almost good as new.

I tripped down the road next day, as promised, uneasy but with a sense of mission. But Stella was worse, it seemed, too bad even to judge the merits of the new little doll. I told Kit about it before dropping off to sleep that night and she murmured something incomprehensible. 'She may be better tomorrow,' I suggested, 'I'll try again. Mrs Turberfield said she wanted me to come.' Suddenly it seemed very important, and for good measure I added Stella's name to my list of folks at the end of my prayers. Kit looked uneasy, but agreed it was the right thing to do. 'Only... well, she *has* been ill for a long time' she

added. I was surprised for I had not thought so. 'How
long?', I queried. 'Oh, about two years, Pet, on and off
... up and down ... you know how it is.'

I supposed I did. I got earache on and off, but it was
alright now. I'd had a bad patch when I was five years
old and been in hospital and had my tonsils out, and
never got around to starting school until I was all of six
years old. So I supposed I knew how it was. But it was
alright eventually, I told Kit. Doctors could do anything, I
ruminated, especially ours who had once been a chemist's
messenger boy. Somebody told us he had delivered
medicine to a rich old lady's house and she had taken him
up and got him through medical college. Now he was one
of our best, Mother had said, for she had tremendous
faith in him and never begrudged the five shillings she
had to find for him every time he came.

Musing confidently upon our own doctor's abilities, I
felt reassured and drowsed off. So I never heard the
hurried footsteps of Stella's father coming down the entry
alongside Tudor House, nor the clop clop of the pony and
trap that brought the doctor on another midnight
rendezvous to the little cottage behind it. Stella died in
the wee small hours without regaining consciousness.

Mrs Turberfield invited me to represent Stella's friends
at the funeral service, and though I had a hollow feeling
inside on that day I was uneasily conscious of a sense of
importance struggling to the fore when I reported to the
cottage at the appointed time.

Gravely Mrs Turberfield, in unaccustomed black, asked
me if I would like to go up and see Stella. I felt it would
be unworthy of me to refuse, having been asked specially
to the funeral. I had never been to one before and
supposed it was the proper thing. I followed others who
were already ascending the familiar stairway.

Stella lay so very still in the small elm coffin that I too
felt transfixed as I stood a few feet away in the room with
its drawn curtains. The curious yellow tinge was still
there upon her features; her lips were slightly parted and
the small teeth that showed seemed to gleam as though
polished. The deep auburn hair, thicker and straighter
than mine, had been carefully brushed to each side of her
face and just touched her shoulders. She wore a white
satin gown which reached to her feet. But finally it was
upon her small hands, folded over her breast, that I
focussed my gaze. I glimpsed a slight discoloration beneath

the finger nails and my heart was wrung with an awful pity, mingled with fear. This wasn't *really* Stella!

'Just like a little doll,' breathed a neighbour reverently. I was utterly silenced. I don't suppose she expected an answer, but I (normally so ready with my tongue) could not have mustered one if my life – God help me – depended on it.

I saw the likeness to some extent, but I knew instinctively that I would never choose a doll like this. The terrible, unnatural stillness overwhelmed me. She had lain still and quiet when I last saw her a few days earlier, but this... this was different.

We returned to the living room below, leaving only an elderly man in a formal morning suit in the room with her. I found I was shaking a little and had a job to negotiate the few stairs where they narrowed and curved, but soon we were back in the familiar living room downstairs and I noticed the big kettle was singing on the blackleaded range. Compassionately now Mrs Turberfield pressed me to take a cup of tea and busied herself in the preparation of it while I sat silently at the big, scrubbed table at which we had played ludo and tiddleywinks.

Mrs Turberfield came across with her brown teapot and poured out several cups of the hot sweet liquid. Then automatically – as she had been doing for weeks past – she picked up the nearest cup and saucer and made for the door at the foot of the stairs. It was not until she raised her free hand to the latch that she realized her error and turned back to those of us who had wordlessly watched her do it. Her thin, angular features crumpled. We cried then, all of us, and felt better for it.

I did not drink my own cup of tea, after all. In some strange, incomprehensible way it seemed as if to do so would be taking advantage of... of Stella, I supposed. It is curious how guilty you can feel, just because you *are* alive and well.

I had a lot of food for thought as I lay sleepless for a long time that night in the bed I now occupied next to Kit's I tried to concentrate on the attractions of Heaven, but in spite of my good Gospel Hall upbringing, the streets of gold seemed infinitely less appealing at that moment than the solid pavements of Friar Street, and the company of angels, in prospect, a poor substitute for that of Kit and the rest of my folks. I did not hit it off all that well with people, but... well... they were *people*.

It was then that a startling fear crossed my mind –
could there possibly be *room enough* for us all in Heaven?
After all, there must be thousands and thousands of good
folk already there from previous generations, let alone our
own. I was filled with foreboding. God could not possibly
go on catering for so many even allowing for the
outrageously obvious fall-outs like thieves, robbers and
murderers.

I stole a glance across to Kit's bed, but she appeared
to be motionless, sleeping. I felt a choking sensation, but
some over-riding principle of compassion kept me silent. I
must not mention this fear to Kit... or to anybody... not
even to my father, who took most things in his small
stride. Perhaps nobody had ever thought of this before? I
would be doing a terrible disservice even to ask about it –
it was so overwhelming.

It was, mercifully, a long time before I learned about
the whirling galaxies that also occupy the universe, and
reversed my anxieties in case there was, after all, too
much room for us to safely find each other on the Other
Side. Perhaps, like most of mankind, I wanted a God who
was big enough to cope but small enough to care.

Come to think of it, a God who is tailored to your own
requirements is no God at all.

CHAPTER 5

Porridge Oats & Bluebells

But for Ruth, daughter of the blind basket-maker, I might never have savoured the dubious delight of sleeping on a straw palliasse, nor solved the mystery of the reef-knot.

Ruth's mother, Lizzie Waldron, lived with her parents in the section of Greyfriars nearest to my father's shop. Though blind from birth, Lizzie conducted her own cottage industry as basket weaver and furniture repairer, combined with a personal collection and delivery service, on foot, without inflicting so much as a single bruise on other pedestrians.

The blind are at the mercy of us all, observation-wise, but I think Miss Waldron would not have minded my curious gaze had she known how fascinated I was at her daily glide past our shop, skilfully circumnavigating our outside display and bearing aloft on her left shoulder a damaged or just-repaired cane-seated chair. The constant, agreeable smile on Lizzie's listening face indicated an outlook containing no resentment at her lot, which was undoubtedly mitigated by the possession of a daughter with an air of indefinable charm, a surprisingly cultured voice and a pair of smokey-grey eyes that did service for them both.

Ruth was a Girl Guide officer who liaisoned with St Helen's Brownie Pack. She cajoled me into enrolment and ultimately carried me off under canvas, with the rest of the local pack of course. It was then that I met Farmer Taylor of Abbotswood Farm, who came to laugh and chat with us, and to regale the pack with his delightful, manly rendering of:

In Dublin' s fair city... where the girls are so pretty,
'Twas there I set eyes on sweet Mollie Malone,
As she wheeled her wheelbarrow, through streets
            broad and narrow,
Crying cockles and mussels, alive! alive-O!

Seated at the top end of our trestle table - the barn served as our Brownies' Mess - with me perched upon his knee and a big wooden spoon in his right hand, he beat time for the chorus and signalled for us to join in. This we did with gusto:

Alive, alive-o-o! Alive, alive-o-o!
Singing cockles and mussels, alive, alive-o!

How I came to be singled out for the privilege of the farmer's lap I do not know, but with all eyes upon the big, white-whiskered face and all hearts captivated by the mood of the moment, I know I would not have changed places with a soul in the world - not even with Olga Evans who was also on the camp and well endowed with sweets from her mother's shop.

The ballad climaxed, as you may know, in the early demise of Sweet Mollie Malone so that in time she became no more than a legend, a memory... a ghost with the faint echo of 'Cockles and mussels...' lingering on the empty air.

It was not only the blue woodsmoke from the dying camp fire that made my eyes water. I blinked hard and took refuge in the thought that Dublin was a long way off - over the sea. Ireland was another country where they believed in leprechauns, toadstools and wishing wells. They kissed the Blarney Stone and wore red cloaks over emerald green dresses with white aprons, to dance the Irish Jig.

Lost in introspection I had missed the cause of poor Mollie's fever and wondered apprehensively how it happened. Had she gone about without shoes, lived overlong on potatoes, or fallen into a peat bog? Ireland was full of them. It couldn't happen here, could it? We don't have bogs... But we had a river, Heaven help us!

Then I remembered the poem Mrs Paterson was trying to drum into us at the Undenominational School - 'The Reaper'. All about a wistful old man with a sickle, who gathered souls and was not content to take only the old and the ailing. When challenged on this point by some intrepid spirit, he had replied in the words which would forever remain in my mind:

> *Shall I have naught that is fair? said He,*
> *Naught but the bearded grain?*

Put like that it was a fair question.

Ten years later I was to recall that couplet with a poignancy that was almost beyond bearing. Today it was a small cloud on the distant horizon, glimpsed through the open door of a crowded barn.

Ah well, if you have to come to terms with griefs and heartbreaks that lurked somewhere out there beyond the patches of evening mist which drifted over hedges and ditches, where better to do so than here, in this warm barn, snuggled against the rough tweed of a big man's shoulder? I could not have known it, but maybe I sensed that into the character of this bluff songster were woven the accumulated experiences of many seedtimes and harvests, births and deaths, triumphs and disasters. He had trodden the green turf and broken open the red clay with steady fortitude, season by season – and still had a song, and time to laugh and play with a motley crowd of noisy little creatures all clad alike in brown cotton.

Soon the melancholia passed. Brown Owl was consulting her lists. Tawny Owl was preparing the long trestle table for tomorrow's breakfast. Out came the enamel dishes, the scratched, well worn cutlery and the bowl of rich, dark brown sugar that had at last convinced me that there was some subtle difference between porridge and poultice.

* * * * *

Soon came our last day at Camp – the day for races and other contests and for the folks at home to come out and join us by means of the 'blue' bus belonging to Mr Marks. They came to watch and applaud and to be fed on thick buttered slices, paste sandwiches, slab cake – and wasps if they did not keep their eyes open between bites.

For the one and only time in my entire life I won a race. Usually, however great my efforts, my physical prowess was not marked. But this day the short arms and legs which failed me at goalposts fitted much more neatly into a hessian sack marked 'Townsend's Flour Mills' than did the heftier limbs of bigger competitors. There has to be justice somewhere!

I thrust my toes well into the corners, took note of the new limitation in my stride, and then – when the pistol cracked and not a split second before – tripped, bounded and hopped my way to the finishing post where I fell headlong across the line to safety.

Exultant with unaccustomed victory, I went up to receive my prize from the gracious lady in the big straw hat, and was abashed (to say the least) to find I had won a small silver thimble. This little badge of domesticity seemed an unfitting climax to an event so virile.

So at last, reclaimed to the bosoms of our respective families, we left Brown Owl and her handmaids to complete the packing of tents, crocks, pots and primus stoves on to the big open dray standing by. We went home in Marks's Blue Bus manned by Sylvia Marks, the proprietor's daughter. Nobody riding behind Sylvia – despite her airy-fairy name and that there were so few lady drivers around – would have the slightest qualm about the prospects of a safe arrival. Sylvia's sturdy shoulders beneath the brown denim overall seemed purpose-built for responsibility; her impassive features conveyed without a quiver of doubt that she knew just what she was about. She finally deposited us, bag and baggage, into the recessed area of the Cornmarket, right in front of King Charles' House.

King Charles House c. 1900

I looked up at it with a new affection as if I had been away for years. Here Charles Stuart had fled into hiding after the Battle of Worcester nearly three hundred years ago. I was glad to be back in the Faithful City, so named (I had been told) because of its loyalty to the Stuarts. I was glad our forbears stood by him in his adversity and smuggled him out to escape the Roundheads and wait for better times. I was confident that the blood which gave Red Hill its name flowed in a good cause.

How anybody could have chosen to fight for Oliver Cromwell I could not conceive, having glimpsed the effigy that was supposed to be his head, nailed by the ears above the entrance to our Guildhall. In my mind the Roundheads were equated with the Communists of our day. Look what happened to Charles I! If the Roundheads had continued long to have their way, we might all have been slaving like the Russians, of whom I had heard that even their women worked on the roads.

I had no fancy for a future with a pick and shovel, and the small seeds of my Toryism took firmer root. By now my ruminations had brought me home, tired and ready for a 'normal' bed. A palliasse is alright in an emergency, or when on a journey to some distant land, but not, I

thought, for regular use. Kit, being one who liked her
comfort, fully agreed and welcomed me back.

For a number of children in our locality 'Grandma'
Browning held the key to the Open Road, though she
herself never seemed to venture further than the
interesting area of pavement which fronted her second
hand furniture mart in Wylds Lane. Chained to her fence,
alongside other goods, was her stock of secondhand
bicycles – for hire at sixpence per hour.

What joy it was, on a Saturday afternoon, to amass the
necessary sum, sally forth down Charles Street, passing

the Gospel Hall and the row of tiny tenement homes and
skirting the Apollo Cinema, to reach Wylds Lane. It was
well to get there early in the hope of finding a bike
entirely suited to one's pedalling power. 'Now look for an
18" frame – ask Mrs Browning to find one – and be
sensible! No main roads or canal banks, mind!' I was
cautioned before setting out. To this I had to agree,
which was not easy for an impressionable child with
imagination fired by screen dramas at the nearby 'Apollo',
and yearning for adventure.

If all the smaller bikes had gone out before I arrived, I
tried unavailingly to persuade Mrs Browning to let me have
a larger one. 'I can stand on the pedals, Mrs Browning,
and rest on the seat in between and going downhill...' But
the old lady was firm. She knew my folks and though she
may have thought it not a bad thing for a forward,
talkative child to be brought to her knees by
over-exertion, she felt it best that it should not occur
astride one of her hired vehicles, and possibly beneath the
wheels of a passing lorry. I had to wait until somebody
else had completed their full hour's ride.

Fortunately the waiting time provided interesting
diversion. Jack Browning's mother displayed samples of
her furnishings, china, bric-a-brac outside her premises
and some goods which had a fair claim to be labelled
'antique' inside the plate glass windows of her corner
shop. Jack was his mother's buyer, who kept the stock
replenished by judicious use of his shrewd though
fun-loving pair of eyes. What was rather special about
Jack was that though married and a father himself, he
could be nice to other people's children. It predisposed
one to admire his acquisitions.

Challenging though it was to compare these with my
own father's wares in Friar Street, one had to bear in
mind that the Brownings had two distinct advantages.
They had joined the then small community of car owners,
which enabled Jack to get around the country sales and
village homes; and theirs was a 'family business' combining
two generations.

Sometimes I carried messages to Jack, who lived near
his mother's shop in Prince Rupert's Road – so named to
perpetuate the part played by that Stuart prince (nephew
of the ill-fated Charles I) in the Civil War. In some idyllic
way it seemed to me that family support was very
important, and it added human interest to the Battle of

Worcester, fought on this spot in 1651, that Rupert came
to the aid of his Cousin Charles, the Stuart heir apparent,
in an attempt to restore the Monarchy and avenge the
death of Charles' father.

I supposed I ought to favour Cromwell's side in the
Civil War because he was a Puritan and shared the views
of the Plymouth Brethren at the Gospel Hall about theatres
and other worldly pleasures. But I was firmly prejudiced
in favour of poor King Charles I who was only four feet
eleven inches tall. It was terrible to think the Roundheads
took upon themselves to shorten him by a head. I could
never think of that big, burly Puritan without resentment.

Which was probably why, when at last I got astride my
hired bike and pedalled my way uphill to Perry Wood's
lower slopes, I gave some credence to that curious legend
about Cromwell having met up there with the Devil and
making a pact with him in order to secure his wretched
victory at Worcester. I was never able to locate the actual
tree in the wood under which this was supposed to have
happened, but viewed them all with apprehensive interest.
I knew of a more recent, authentic drama here for one of
our neighbourhood children, leader of a band of noisy,
adventurous boys with whom I often wanted to play despite
my sister Naomi's ladylike disdain, had been roped to a
tree in a Sherwood Forest mock-up. With a fire of
brushwood kindled around him, the game had got out of
hand and poor Alfie Beswick was burned to death before
rescue could be summoned!

Despite the haunts, legendary or real, Perry Wood had
its great attractions. In retrospect I feel again the
breathtaking wonder of the carpet of bluebells which
surfaced above the rough turf between the trees.
Unrestricted in those days, I picked with careless
abandon, lowered them into a carrier bag and hung them
over Mrs Browning's handlebars to beautify our livingroom
above the shop (we had no garden). But more precious
even than they, were the tiny violets, both blue and
white, which nestled modestly beneath the foliage at the
foot of the trees. They were fewer and harder to find,
which makes for value in this curious world.

I sought them out with care and studied them with
deliberate respect, bearing home just a few to give them
brief pride of place. Unbidden, from some recess in my
memory, Gray's Elegy came to mind, probably because of
its best known couplet, which I had recently been taught

by the grave and dignified Miss Barter in Form IV...

Full many a flower is born to blush unseen,
And waste its sweetness on the desert air.

I assumed Thomas Gray was registering a lament because
of human potential unfulfilled. The beauty of the words
was emphasized in the stillness of the wood at a time when
I thought fame and success were so desirable.

Later I realized that the Elegy was possibly stirred
from my sub-conscious mind because of its brief but
expressive link-up with the character which had been
dominating my thoughts. Was the poet really intending to
convey that the fulfilment of ambition may prove a mixed
blessing? for he wrote:

Some mute inglorious Milton here may rest
'Some Cromwell guiltless of his country's blood'

The meadow at the foot of Perry Wood provided easier
gradients for cyclists and one could skim the surface and
perform 'figures of eight' with more abandon than
anywhere else. The cowslips and ladysmock, and the
ubiquitous buttercup all flourished anew each year and
provided less melancholy pleasure.

Then I would grow anxious that my hour might be up
and, not then possessing my own timepiece, I would turn
my wheels back down the rough track to Wylds Lane
reassured in the knowledge that my return would be the
easy, downhill progress past the terraced villas and the
few shops – but also past the Garibaldi Inn...

Though I hurried by it, giving an extra, unnecessary
spurt to the pedals, I could not resist a sidelong glance at
the Garibaldi, for in that year when I was nine years old
it made the headlines in our local press. Its proprietor,
Ernie Laight, together with his wife and baby son, Bobby,
had been cruelly murdered, while their daughter Joan,
whom I knew slightly and who was a little younger than I
was, somehow slept deeply through it all. The apalling
thing, and one which was incredible to a child who saw
The Law as representing all that was safe and predictable
in life, was that the murders were carried out by a young
police officer who was a customer at the tavern and known
to the family.

Moved as I always was by the dramatic, I had listened

to the discussions of this case between my parents, among others, and heard that P.C. Herbert Burrows had not left the premises at the familiar call of 'Time, Gentlemen, please,' but had concealed himself in the cellar below. His intention was apparently to creep upstairs and help himself to the takings in the hope of slipping away unnoticed and certainly unsuspected.

The pity of it was that Joan's father, after clearing the place up, had found it necessary to go down the cellar for some purpose. The young policeman was discovered and the landlord shot as he reached the foot of the steps. Apparently hearing commotion, his wife came bravely down with her candle, and met the same fate, falling face downwards by the side of her dying husband. As he fled up to the bar, the policeman heard the cry of their two-year-old son in his bed, ran upstairs and silenced Bobby forever with a shattering blow to the head. Joan slept on, unawares.

Incredibly, even now the killer fulfilled his purpose and robbed the place, then, possibly as an afterthought, descended the cellar steps again and made an ineffective attempt to set fire to the building. His escape was brief, for just at the time when the crime was discovered by the cleaner on the following morning, he betrayed himself by an unwise remark to a fellow constable, revealing knowledge of the crime before it had been officially reported.

On a cold January morning in 1926 Herbert Burrows paid for his sins on the gallows at Gloucester Gaol. It was a melancholy affair on which to ruminate in one's childhood, and yet quaintly it was an apparently irrelevant remark by the Prosecuting Counsel which lingered in my fanciful memory. In mitigation, the constable's Defence lawyer had pleaded that Burrows was 'an infant in law' for he was below 21 years of age and merely a probationary constable. Contemptuously dismissing this plea in his final address to the jury, the Prosecutor referred to the hapless offender as: 'Then this *'infant'* – this *six foot infant* – proceeded to...' etc., etc.

Perhaps, after all, I thought – for the first time – it is best to be small and insignificant, and not to draw attention to yourself and never, never to hit the headlines! And certainly P.C. Burrows's fate was a salutary warning to any sinner whose tongue wagged too freely...

It was reassuring to hear that the culprit had what our Gospel Hall would call a deathbed repentance, though he was denied that literal physical comfort. He is reputed to have said at the last: 'If you can, forgive me, for I am sorry.' Since repentance is so vital, according to the Scriptures, to qualify for forgiveness, this was a very hopeful sign, it seemed to me. I was always glad of hopeful signs.

But what of Joan – she who was most sadly deprived by this triple tragedy? I never saw her again, but understood she went to live with her grandmother. This was surely the next-best-thing. I expected never to face such a dilemma, but when offended with my own immediate 'loved ones' I sometimes purposed to remove myself to my grandparents for good, and even packed my bag once or twice. But always, of course, in the expectation that my folks would repent of whatever they had done, or left undone, to me, and the parental door would swing open again.

I greatly hoped Joan and her grandmother were able to console each other. I thought of them often, particularly when our Mother had the impulse to sing to us her touching ballads of sad partings and grievous loss. One featured a child's lament for his mother. 'Turn your face to the west, Daddy...' (I think were the words). In memory I recall the mental image of a wistful child, nestling confidingly against his father as together they watched the setting sun... and maybe wondered what lay beyond that crimson beauty. Nowadays that song of faithful vigil would be judged to be highly sentimental, and even then I would *never* yield to tears. But I remember still that apalling physical discomfort in my throat as I struggled to regain composure without anybody noticing.

Often, when returning my hired bike to Mrs Browning, I was surprised to hear: 'Time's not up yet – go off for another ten minutes', which I thought very honest of her. She did not display the affability of her son Jack, but I later came to suspect that she gave me a gratuitous extension for my sixpence.

But ultimately it was time to surrender my steed, disengage the carrier of bluebells and bear them triumphantly home. They might possibly last long enough to grace the school windowsill on Monday morning, perhaps? Arranging them then in a glass vase or jar (more

often the latter) I found them still beautiful though their
stems were soft and supple. Consequently their lovely blue
heads drooped, as if confirming that life really is a
curious mixture of pleasure and of pain.

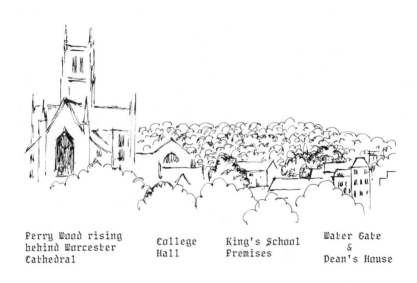

Perrp Wood rising   College   King's School   Water Gate
behind Worcester   Hall   Premises   &
Cathedral   Dean's House

CHAPTER 6

Airs and Graces

'Pale Hands I Love, Beside the Shalima...ar'

It was Miss Ellen's soft soprano, rising and falling on that last syllable. Curled up on the square pouffe in the opposite corner of the room, I glanced up from Kit's copy of 'What Katy did Next' to glimpse the dark head and arched, white neck of the singer. She stood beside Kit at the piano in the recess between the fireplace and the window. The fingers of her right hand, nicely manicured as those of a typist and an engaged girl should be, curved over the corner of the music sheet ready to flick over when Kit gave the nod.

This was Saturday evening in Grandmother's upstairs parlour. By midsummer Miss Ellen would be my aunt for she was going to marry Uncle Reg - and it was plain to see that she was considered an acquisition to the family. All afternoon in this room there had been a tremendous furore of spit and polish, though you would never think so now, with everybody so relaxed amid the curling wreaths of tobacco smoke and the occasional contented pop and puff from the overhead gas mantle which both warmed and illuminated the scene.

Earlier in the day the big table downstairs had been covered with a crisp white damask cloth, and out had come the best white china with the salmon pink edging. Only Grandfather qualified for the special 'moustache cup' to the rim of which was fitted a sort of china filter to keep his long, drooping whiskers from getting mixed up with the tealeaves. The gadget could not have been foolproof, I conjectured, for Grandfather's grey-white moustache was distinctly tipped with reddish brown at each side.

The teatable had been carefully laid with everything in its exact place and everybody schooled into restraint. Uncle Reg - free today from the footplate of the Paddington Express - must not, on any account, be Let Down. He had gone to bring his Young Lady to the feast, traversing our river bridge which had formerly marked the boundary between England and Wales, to fetch her. She was no foreigner though. It appeared she had been born in Tudor House, opposite to Grandfather's shop, so I supposed she and Uncle Reg had been neighbouring toddlers - or should it be toddling neighbours? But now, while many girls went 'into service' for want of better opportunities, Miss Ellen was a Shorthand-Typist, no less.

After tea, which had to include Grandmother's speciality (trifle with damson preserve between the sponge layers and a dash of port wine to add 'body') the company had adjourned to the upstairs parlour and inevitably Kit was seated at her piano, browsing through the sheets of music for family favourites.

'Pale hands I love...' - a most affecting phrase, even if one was inclined to be blasé about romance. What was the

Shalimar? It was somehow connected with the mysterious East which was enough to make it popular for these were the days when everything romantic savoured of the Orient. Rudolph Valentino was the current screen idol and all desirable males of the day were 'sheiks'. This Kit and I had learned from a contralto in the Methodist Choir, to whom a party was no party worth describing unless it could be added: 'And then this sheik came along - Oh--oo!'.

Soon Kit would be following on with her more restrained 'In a Monastery Garden', her rich voice deepening on the mysterious refrain: 'Keyrie Eleison... Keyrie Eleison...' which I supposed to be the canticles sung by monks or friars following in the footsteps of those who, long ago, had paced the cloisters and passageways concealed below this very house.

It was reassuring to have Uncle Walter move across to the fire to add a log to the blaze before crossing resolutely, with a slight cough, over to the piano. We knew his choice would be:

> *There's an old-fashioned house in an old-fashioned*
> *street*
> *In a quaint little old-fashioned town;*
> *There's a street where the cobble stones harras*
> *the feet*
> *As it struggles up hill and then down...*
>
> *And, though to and fro through the world I*
> *must go,*
> *My heart while it beats in my breast,*
> *Where-e're I may roam, To that old-fashioned home*
> *Will fly back like a bird to its nest.*

Then I would look up at the framed photograph on the wall between the two parlour windows and be glad that the three soldier sons there depicted together in khaki all came safely home from the Great War - Uncle Walter from the mud and slaughter of Flanders and Uncle Sidney from captivity at the hands of the cruel Turks. My own little Father, who never so much as crossed the English Channel, earned three stripes in some garrison office and what we children thought for years to be a greater distinction shown by the three shiny metal letters at the shoulder of his tunic. How should we know they merely stood for Army Veterinary Corps?

Half in hope and half in dread I waited for 'Smiling Through', knowing this would signal the inevitable struggle in my throat, for I would see, more clearly than the printed page I pretended to concentrate upon, the image of the lonely, loving widower at the wicket gate, keeping his tryst. But it was good to know that he could conclude:

In all the long years, when the clouds brought their
tears,
Those two eyes of blue, came smiling through...
at me.

Sooner or later Kit would raise our spirits with the sprightly ditty about the Irish colleen whom nothing would tempt into matrimony until her swain had the inspiration to offer a litter of piglets to grace the happy hearth which he hoped to share. It was his triumphant boast which concluded the song:

The little pigs had done it!
Och! The dear little girl!

and I fell to thinking it could be true that the Irish really did have pigs running around their living quarters. Expressed in song it did not sound half so off-putting.

Then it was time for Uncle Reg to walk home his bride-to-be, along the river bank and over the river bridge. Did they pause there, I wondered, to lean over the parapet and recapture the romance of Miss Ellen's song? Maybe the Shalimar *was* a river as I had conjectured. The Severn might not have the mystery of the East, or even the breadth of the nearer Thames, but it is the longest river in England and has its own winding charm.

With the advent of Summer came all the excitement of the wedding, carefully planned, for Miss Ellen was a stickler for detail. It was the first wedding in our family that I could recall and I looked on at the preparations expectantly. She had a chief bridesmaid but might she not want a couple of small ones?

But alas and alack! Mother came back from a consultation about details with a subdued demeanor. We waited for the latest news. She had quite a job mustering the right approach, but eventually it transpired that Miss Ellen wanted only one small bridesmaid from our side of the family, for she had small relations too! '...and this little niece of hers,' confessed Mother hesitantly, 'is a fair haired little girl. So she thinks Naomi would be the best one to pair with her'!

I stared back, disbelievingly. I might not have felt so bad if I had not been fifteen months older than my sister, though the same size, and assumed it to be my natural inheritance to be the pioneer in family events... What was more incredible was that Mother had agreed to this highly unjust arrangement!

She salved her conscience by ordering an identical dress for me so that after the wedding Naomi and I could be paraded on Sundays looking like the twins many people mistook us for.

But what on earth was the use of a bridesmaid dress that would never go down the aisle? I was filled with indignation and refused to be mollified, even when we reported to nearby Lamb's outfitters to select the material. 'It has to be lemon for this one,' explained Mother,

touching my sister's shoulder, 'But I think a deeper shade
for this one, don't you?' She and the assistant eyed my
freckles doubtfully.

'Green, of course, is usually good with auburn...,'
began the salesgirl in the trim black dress, 'but not, I
think, right for a wedding...?' Mother forebore to mention
that my dress would not even *see* the wedding, or that
green was peculiarly appropriate to my attitude. She
conveyed her doubt with a quizzical eyebrow and the
assistant glanced at the laden shelves behind her. 'Ah!
The new Alice Blue – just right for her, I think...' – then
spoiled the effect by adding: 'It will give interest to the
little girl's pale complexion, Madam', so I walked away and
left them to it.

I was beginning to harbour doubts about the reason
given for my rejection, but could not think of an
alternative that brought me less discredit. *I* didn't like the
colour of my hair, either – but it was not my fault! My
sister was fair, demure and winsome with bonny curves.
In our first school play she, who shrank from stardom,
got the title role of 'The Sleeping Beauty'!

'There's one thing for sure,' I informed my mother that
evening, 'I don't put on airs and graces. I'm always the
same,'

Why I regarded this as a virtue I cannot now think.
Mother, tiring of the subject, pronounced it 'old buck' and
insinuated that I had more than enough of it. Moreover
she indicated that the new bride probably shared that
opinion and I was the author of my own misfortunes.

'Anyway,' she added finally, 'You can't have it all
ways. Naomi's got looks. You've got brains. Be satisfied!'

It did not occur to me to doubt this assessment, but at
that moment and many times later I would have traded in a
couple of grammes of 'grey matter' with anybody for a pair
of sparkling eyes.

There seemed nothing more to be said. I crept down
into the now closed shop and hid away in the far corner
behind a satinwood wardrobe, giving myself up to my
chagrin and a horsehair sofa.

It was not that I really wanted to be a bridesmaid, of
course. It was all a lot of nonsense, after all. No bride
needs more than one person to hold her bouquet while the
ring goes on, so all the rest were just for show. But even
so, I should have been given the *chance* to stand down...
At this point I recollected that Uncle Reg was ginger too,

and took satisfaction in the thought that Miss Ellen's offspring could well suffer my fate. Just before the betraying tears came, I was concentrating fiercely on a little patch of woodworm in a back panel of the wardrobe. Then the tiny holes swam into one murky mirage, and I guess it was wormwood that took over, mixed with gall and spiced with spleen... a curious flavour which unhappily may develop an acquired taste!

The evening drew in abruptly. Shadows collected all over the shop. Glass and mirrors here and there glinted dully. I had grown stiff and cold, and pulled myself stealthily to my feet. Not a soul had been down to find out where I was! For all they knew I might be at the bottom of the Severn.

The reflection that looked back at me from the nearest mirror was not reassuring. I flung my head higher and made for the doorway en route for Kit and the refuge of her second floor bedroom. But if they thought I was going to say my prayers that night, they could think again. Life was very unfair. It was odd that such a state of affairs was allowed.

'Jealousy,' says the Good Book, 'is cruel as the grave.' There is no better comparison. Like the grave it divides, separates, isolates... All wrong, of course. All the same, he who fashions the coat of many colours should not take too great a pride in his handiwork.

* * * * *

Ching, Ching Chinaman, muchee muchee sad,
He aflaid, allee tlade velly velly bad.
No one buy, so he cry, 'Shuttee shuttee shop!'
Ching, Ching Chinaman – Chop! Chop! Chop!

Mother was amusing one of the little ones, giving the little ditty her usual beguiling emphasis and with not the slightest intention to communicate racial prejudice. If the words conveyed his actual situation, Ching Ching Chinaman was no worse or better off than most other traders in Friar Street and Sidbury in the second half of the nineteen twenties.

Guiltily I was reminded that this was the day to collect my grandfather's collars from the Chinese Laundry up the road. Sometimes Grandmother sent other garments, but the regular consignment was the pack of separate collars which could be detached and laundered independent of a man's shirt. So I sped up there and found things going on much as usual. Judging by the shelves filled with piles of freshly ironed clothing, and the aroma of slightly scorched linen, all was well with Ah Wong anyway, though you could not tell from the inscrutable expression of the faces of both the proprietor and his lady. You produced the little coloured scrap of paper with its peculiar hieroglyphics and Mrs Ah Wong (presumably) located your package at once. I wondered how they came to leave the land of pagodas, shrines and rickshaws for the grey dust and concrete of Sidbury, but there was no chance of knowing.

Tripping back down to Grandfather's, it was reassuring to cross the road to Ernie Wellesbury's shop window, to study the charcoal portrait on the easel which would be his tribute, and an excellent one, to the forthcoming visiting 'royal'. Having a resident artist opposite to us added to the lustre of our locality and to the sense of satisfaction at being born at the heart of the British Empire. It was the Duke of York, the King's second son and his charming Scottish Duchess, who were shortly to honour our city with a visit – and everybody was busy unrolling bunting and Union Jacks in readiness.

Mr Wellesbury was charming and courteous even to an inquisitive child. His artistry combined with Rudyard Kipling's poetry to promote a sense of wellbeing and what then seemed a commendable national pride. This was vastly reinforced when the Great Day came and our cheering citizens lined the High Street pavements three and four deep, despite the fact that we scarcely got a glimpse of the Duchess's feather boa between the hats and ears of the early birds in front of us. Had we but known it, we would have done better to spend the day hobnobbing with Aunt Trudie and her daughters Josephine and Monica at the little cottage behind the Powick Mill where Uncle Will worked. They stood, almost alone, on Powick Bridge to wave the Duke and Duchess on to Malvern. The royal car slowed, and the family were accorded a gracious acknowledgement and a charming smile as only the former Lady Elizabeth Bowes-Lyon could bestow so winningly. Later, Aunt Trudie described the scene graphically, as was her wont.

Our patriotism and sense of national identity was reinforced later that year at the Gospel Hall Sunday School prizegiving, which carried the additional reassurance that God was in his heaven. The scholars' items following the distribution of the awards were impressive, none more so than the Kipling poem given forth with great aplomb and rolling of the R's by a tall, slim dark boy who lived around the corner, below the Gospel Hall, and was only a few months my senior. His sister, a lively, smiling young woman, was a close friend of Kit's and was sometimes the server behind the counter of our local fish and chip shop in a section of the Greyfriars building. She was smiling, jolly (and generous too we thought with our portions), so we silently willed her younger brother to do well knowing she and Kit, somewhere in the audience at our rear, would be on tenterhooks.

The reciter's confident, trusting, blue eyes gazed over our heads to the wall at the rear as he posed his big question:

Where are you going to, all you Big Steamers,
With England's own coal up and down the salt seas?

and, of course, was obliged to supply his own reassuring answer:

We are going to fetch you your bread and your
butter
Your beef, pork and mutton, eggs, apples and cheese!

He must have been a star performer that year for not only did he impress these lines indelibly upon Naomi's memory and mine (we repeated them to each other at intervals for months afterwards), but he presently came up with a second item, designed to convince one that greatness did not only consist of exploits on the high seas and beyond. By some odd coincidence his second poem began with a question, too:

What can a little chap do?

The name of the author and the conclusion of the poem escape me now, but the accompanying illustration in Princess Mary's Gift Book, which found its way among a job lot into our shop just afterwards, spoke volumes. At the kerb of a busy thoroughfare stood a small Boy Scout, poised to pilot across the road a wounded soldier with

bandaged head who leaned trustingly upon the small
shoulder.

The earnestness with which the verses were conveyed
not only added to our enjoyment, but was proved to be
sincere. In succeeding years the boy chose to learn
Esperanto (the language which it was hoped would become
common to all), to champion the cause of the League of
Nations as it was formed, to volunteer to serve King and
Country... and incidentally, ten years later, to ask me to
marry him. Alas, all of these aspirations proved less
satisfying than he expected.

Scouting movements gained ground rapidly and Uncle
Sidney's second son, Fred, chose to ally himself to the
Boys' Brigade. After a few months initiation he nobly put
himself, and his close friend Bob, at our family's disposal
by organising a Family Camp in which we could spend our
Summer Holiday under canvas in the meadows of Farmer
Tooby at Powick. Not having the choice of going
elsewhere, we settled for this and, leaving Father to cope
alone with his shop for a couple of weeks in August, we
somehow contrived to get ourselves transported thither,
passing over the narrow Powick Bridge to enter the field.
Fortunately the turf which had once been stained crimson
with the blood of Roundheads and Royalists was now a
fresh, springy green apart from the odd patches one must
expect when sharing territory with cattle.

Since Cousin Fred found his future bride at a nearby
cottage, it is possible he was not entirely motiveless in
selecting Farmer Tooby's field, whilst the fair, curly head
and lithe figure of Cousin Fred's ally and fellow-Brigader
might have had some slight bearing in encouraging others
of us to cope again with straw palliasses. No doubt our
mother was influenced in her agreement to join the camp
because of her sister Trudie's close proximity in the
cottage behind the Mill. Although we were catering for
ourselves for those two weeks in Tooby's orchards, the
goodwill of nearby loved ones had a distinct advantage –
though the length of two fields was a fair distance to run
if you found yourself bereft of salt after Cousin Fred had
expended his lung power coaxing the potatoes to the boil.

Having got us installed, the 'Brigaders' responded
nobly to the call of duty to us and to Fred's two small
sisters, May and Winifred, who had tagged along, though
it was a little disconcerting to find that the slim, alert
figures wearing immaculate navy blue with spotless white

lanyards and gleaming brass trumpets bear little resemblance to the dishevelled creatures who crawl through half-opened tent flaps in the early morning and set up an immense clatter with the mess tins.

There was not much danger this time of developing home-sickness, since most of our nearest and dearest were on hand. Mother and Aunt Trudie, at times joined by other sisters with their brood travelling out on the Midland Red Bus, got together, caught up with the news and compared their children's illnesses. The topic was inspired by the recent recovery of our smallest cousin, Monica, from a dire malady. The details were so fresh in Aunt Trudie's mind that her discourse held pride of place, though Aunt Alice made it plain – more by her facial expression than words – that it was still her opinion that their Trevor had had a much narrower squeak the year before, his illness having baffled diagnosis until almost too late. I thought it curious that people seemed to take pride in maladies seldom or never heard of before. After all, one has a better chance with measles, with which a doctor has had plenty of practice.

Uncle Will spent his day keeping the wheels of the Mill turning. Fred and Bob deposited May and Winifred with us whilst they went off and did whatever Boys' Brigaders were supposed to do. We others could paddle and sunbathe at leisure, for the shallows of the Teme were inviting. Cousin Jo, when she came across from the cottages, declined our invitation to join us and settled on a groundsheet and pillows with a book. She lived alongside the Teme and something you see every day is apt to lose its novelty. In all probability seaside dwellers are similarly disadvantaged.

Then came the moment when I trod on a wasp expiring in the shallows. He must have been coming up for the third time when, in the absence of a convenient straw, he clutched the small toe of my left foot. The pain was excruciating. I had been brought up on the premise that only babies cry, so I found great difficulty in convincing others of the depth of my suffering. All they seemed concerned about was to ensure the wasp had no successors. I rocked backwards and forwards on the sunbaked, unyielding turf, but beyond putting out a near-empty marmalade jar to catch my wasp's mourners, nobody did a thing. Then - oh joy - I recalled a remedy.

'A bluebag!' I yelled, hopefully, 'Have we got a bluebag?' By some peculiar oversight it had not occurred to Mother to pack a bluebag with the camp stores! Hopping on one foot, I urgently besought Cousin Jo to fetch relief from their cottage. But Jo, well into an enthralling chapter of somebody's adventures, had no mind to share mine. 'Don't be silly,' she chided, loftily, 'Rub it - hard!' and went back to her page. How she ever aspired to become a Nursing Sister in later years I cannot imagine - much less to become the Ministering Angel of London's West India Docks and open her clinic to seafarers from all over the world!

The fierce sunshine of that day was the prelude to a thunderstorm that night. That the tents stayed upright can only be put down to the excellent training of the Boys' Brigade. The rain belted down in torrents; thunder roared above us and lightning streaked across the sky. Beyond the occasional shouted response to enquiries as to our welfare, emanating from the Brigaders' little sleeping tent, we lay huddled on our pallets and tried to think reassuring thoughts.

'Whatever you do,' our Father had urged us from his vast experience with the Veterinary Corps and the Territorials, 'If it should rain, don't raise your heads against the canvas or it will come pouring in at that point.' Seeing that this was a bell tent borrowed from the Territorials, we trusted his judgement and were thankful we were not six-footers. If all eight of us had our feet near the centre pole and spread around starwise, we had a good chance of avoiding touching the perimeter. Just occasionally life offers these slight advantages to the short in stature.

The storm continued for what seemed hours. Mother,
who had a strong stomach for most challenges in life,
became distinctly queasy, and communicated her
predicament to me for I was nearest to the exit. Finally 'I
shall have to go,' she said and snaked out through the
tent flap in an undignified crawl. Fortunately the lightning
was retreating and she was able to emerge into the
apalling downpour unobserved. What happened after that is
anybody's guess because you don't ask a person that sort
of thing. I was thankful to hear the swish of her
returning form, soaked but relieved, when a fresh terror
encompassed us.

It was a low throb and there seemed to be lights
flashing around in all directions. 'What on earth...?' began
Mother, and I hushed her for I had visions of an
unwanted visit from a flying object and had no wish to
attract its occupants to our tent flap. Or... it might be
the mill, I thought, terrified. Something's given way. The
Teme has burst its banks! We shall all be drowned and
swept away! The persistent throb loomed nearer and the
lights flashed through the canvas - *our* canvas - then a
klaxon horn piped through the darkness and a gruff,
familiar voice tersely and somewhat inappropriately
demanded: 'Anybody at home here?'

It was Uncle Sidney and Aunt Margaret who had forced
their way over streaming roads and ploughed across two
soggy fields in their old brown Ford coupé in a rescue bid
that would have done Grace Darling credit. They had come
primarily of course for their two small daughters though in
the event May, the elder, elected to stay with the troops.
Winifred was disposed to treat her rescuers very coolly
and would have chosen likewise, but her parents were not
prepared to write off this hazardous expedition as a social
call. Uncle Sidney might have relented after ascertaining
that his offspring were safe and reasonably sound in the
hands of the Boys' Brigade, but Aunt Margaret was a
woman of firm purpose. So to save more ado, for it is an
exhausting business to carry on an argument in such
circumstances, their last-born was offered up as a
sacrificial lamb, hauled like a waterproofed mummy through
the flap of the tent, and deposited in some miraculous
fashion inside the coupé.

We watched the operation through the stealthily lifted
outer rim of our bit of tent, conveyed the information that
the rest of us were alright thank you, and let them go,

bumping and squelching their way across the sodden turf
(and patches of cow dung) until the tiny red rear light
was lost to our sight negotiating Powick Bridge.

With hindsight one could dwell with some pride upon the
heroic though somewhat brusque stance adopted by our
uncle in a world where few people possessed anything on
wheels not pulled by a horse or pedalled with the feet.
The sight of him had done us good, as had his
non-committal tones conveying the impression that the
world was not yet coming to an end. Few of us were quite
ready for that event, despite the Boy Scouts' motto.

Powick Bridge

Kit and Mrs Kate Lawrence

CHAPTER 7

Of Vexations and Vocations

I NEVER THOUGHT of Kit as 'a cripple'. She and I detested the term as a description of a person. She was just... Kit. Her disability was incidental.

Which is not to say she did not mind about it – though, as a child spending long months in Birmingham and London hospitals, she took it pretty well. These were the days when families were very firmly discouraged from visiting children's wards, even if they could muster the wherewithal to travel the distances and the courage to tackle the Ward Sisters. Yet Kit did not appear to develop a neurosis from the deprivation, not even when later sympathizers would lament her inability to run about and play like other children. 'Frankly, pet,' she once confided to me, 'I couldn't really see what all the fuss was about. It was rather nice to be petted, carried around in comfort and to watch others wearing themselves out whatever the weather.' She was a good spectator.

But it was in the teens and twenties that it mattered most. Kit had a strong and lively personality, which rather precluded her from being the meek and patient sufferer one is supposed to be. In fact, if she tried to move too quickly, took a toss and landed on the ground, she felt pretty mad about it. If the folk then at hand did not get the gist of her thoughts, those at home did later!

Once she got walking aids suited to her needs, Kit plunged into a variety of pursuits, though she never felt the necessity of martyring herself by Earning a Living under herioc circumstance, which is supposed to be necessary to one's self esteem. I confess this added to her attraction in my view. Not having to 'go to work' seemed a step up in the social scale of the nineteen twenties. It also meant that she was generally on hand when you wanted her, instead of wasting all the good hours of the day behind some closed door, desk, counter or machine. True, Grandmother had hopefully despatched her to Miss Darke's secretarial establishment to be initiated into the mysteries of Pitman's Shorthand and touch typing. Subsequently a large and dictatorial Miss Baskerville, wearing a brown denim overall with a row of pens in the top pocket, descended upon us and bore Kit off to McCowen's Leather Emporium up the road, where Friar Street joined Sidbury. Here Kit's prospects were enhanced because Mr McCowen was the merchant from whom Grandfather purchased his strong leather sheets for shoe repairing. Furthermore Grandfather went fishing with the proprietor, who was now developing a second line of business for the benefit of anglers and himself in particular.

But alas! This weight of influence made little

difference. It was a painful time for all concerned until
Miss B. gave Kit up as a bad job. Kit was 'piping her eye'
when they brought her home, probably in mortal terror of
Miss Baskerville, who seemed to wield more authority than
the boss. Later Kit could discuss it without rancour. 'I
really am a fool,' she would say, with practically no
regret, for she found the admission saved people from a
lot of disappointment.

Then she and I would breathe again, and allow
ourselves to relax with some more interesting diversion.
That is, until Great Aunt Emily came along, on a week's
visit from Gloucester.

Some years earlier, under circumstances never divulged
to me, Aunt Em had become widowed at the age of
eighteen. Maybe this had inclined her to the conclusion
that you could not trust to chance in this world, and it
became her mission in life to turn Kit into a seamstress.
Hopefully Grandmother lashed out on the latest Singer
Drophead Sewing Machine.

Fabrics never did become the ruling passion in Kit's
life. We pored over the manual together but never quite
got the hang of why the top row of stitching deceived you
into false security, to be dashed when you turned your
material over. Then it looked for all the world as if you
were bent on spinning an elongated spider's web. We
practised on the renovation of worn sheets by trying the
sides-to-middle method, but made slow progress.

Spurred on by the hope that a more interesting subject
might inspire our latent skill, we undertook to make
Grandmother a dress in readiness for her summer holiday.
However frugally she might live in other directions,
Grandmother had a weakness for seasides and funfairs,
which seemed rather odd. She was never one for gay
abandon otherwise.

Trustingly she sallied forth to Russell & Dorrell's and
treated herself to four yards of brown floral silk and a
paper pattern depicting a demure, long-sleeved garment
which would have done credit to a school-marm. Over this
we laboured for days. Despite occasional moments of
anguish, the final result would have been beyond reproach
if we had not had the misfortune to cut out both sleeves
for the same arm – and no material left to rectify it. We
hadn't the heart to take Grandmother into our confidence,
with the hours ticking away to the moment of her
departure.

The easy solution would have been to insert one sleeve inside out, but the flowers on the reverse side had a definitely faded look even in artificial light. We feared this might not escape the notice of Grandmother's fellow guests when she passed the marmalade at Ramsgate, so somehow we cajoled the second sleeve into the vacant armhole, right side outside. It looked slightly askew on its hanger in the mahogany wardrobe, but Grandmother was never one for waste and got resolutely into it. I doubt whether she could lift her arm above elbow level, and her skill on the Promenade hoopla stall must definitely have been impaired. To her lasting credit, she never even said so.

Kit had rather more success with the toy-and-fancy-goods-stall which my father opened in the local Market Hall off the nearby Shambles, and made new friends into the bargain. There is a comradeship between stallholders that is lacking in shop traders. Ethel, who sold hats two stalls away, was Kit's best ally and when they had no customers, many a happy hour was whiled away trying on Ethel's stock. They were joined on occasions by the girl whose mother had a produce stall in the next aisle. Convent-educated, Daisy was a bit above stallholding herself, but her cheerful chat provided a welcome diversion for Kit and Ethel and somehow all three seemed to be on hand when the good-looking, dignified rent collector made his rounds. All their hopes were dashed when he married the daughter of the owner of an imposing emporium nearby, but Kit made a lifelong friend in Daisy Tolley.

Daisy's mother was an acquisition to any traders' market. She had a regal bearing and a rich, deep voice which gave significance to everything she said. She wore close-fitting velvet hats enveloped in fine net veils which covered her face and tied beneath her firm, well controlled chin. She drove her goods to market in her own horse and trap, and never did a pair of well gloved hands wield reins and whip with more dexterity.

It goes without saying that all her wares were home produced from her spacious, farmhouse kitchen in the nearby village of Norton - chutneys, jellies, jams, cream and butter churned in her vast, cool dairy. Piles of new-laid eggs, oven-ready poultry and her stock of gorgeous Madeira cakes made with her own butter completed the display. In fact I established a close acquaintance with Mrs Tolley's produce, and another liaison with Kit, by helping Mrs Tolley on Saturday mornings - and was intrigued with the brisk momentum of life around us. When not busy, I wandered off for a closer look.

To Market... to Market

Pratley's China Stall dominated the central aisle. A vociferous young man held shrill discourse on his wares, and was not averse to smashing the odd article or two to emphasize his point, that he was absolutely throwing away his goods, and money was his least concern. Beyond him the novelty stall beckoned and intrigued. Balloons, festoons and monkeys-on-a-string were most popular. If you never savoured the pleasurable power of pressing together the two slim sticks which flicked aloft the furry grey monkey, then you will not have been rewarded by watching him leap over and over as his little bell celebrated his share of the enterprise.

Near to Kit's stall a charming old man with pure white hair and whiskers, ruddy cheeks and a magnificent smile ran the Colporteur's stall selling Bibles and religious literature, text cards and Bible-picture puzzles. His lightest reading was contained in the 'Lily Series' of slim paperbacks. Fiction and romance they offered, but the more startling red covers of magazines on the adjoining bookstall did tantalize the imagination more. Their heroines gazed up with wide eyes in excited wonder, fear or pathos and full red lips usually parted with some emotion which could only be traced in the pages of the 'Red Star' or 'Poppy'. The white-haired Mr Yelland's gorgeous smile and his long acquaintance with my father and the Gospel Hall persuaded me to let conscience be my guide and choose the pale blue printed cover of the latest 'Lily series' from his stall, and bear it back to Mrs Tolley's produce counter.

All in all, those Saturday mornings were quite an education of which I might have been robbed by foolish pride. Being handmaiden to a stallholder might not appear to be much of a status, but when the stallholder was Mrs Tolley the situation was redeemed. Mrs Tolley was my grandmother's friend and they spent days together on the farm. In fact Mrs T. had been my grandparents' landlady, for she owned some of the Friar Street properties. Later my grandparents were able to purchase their premises from her, largely, I gathered (from overhearing those fascinating snatches of conversation not meant for one's ears), as a result of Grandmother's thrift rather than through Grandfather's adventures with the Tote.

So I was associated with the management, which puts a much better complex on things in the same way that the self-employed can stoop to lowly tasks with dignity. One can do a menial task without loss of face if nobody *tells* you to do it. So, even when I picked up the big wicker basket and set out by bus to deliver the uncollected orders, I could do so with aplomb. It gave me entrance into the homes of the idle rich and to discover what went on Below Stairs where I was plied with lemonade and jam tarts.

Most of the kitchen staff appeared well fed and content with their lot, though I was told of one who, denied her evening off at the last moment and thus forced to forego her date with the coalman because The Quality were Having Company, spat into the soufflé mix three times as she beat it savagely with her wooden spoon. Perhaps it ought not to be mentioned (unfortunately one cannot whisper in print), but it may serve to comfort those who have been forced, all their lives long, to cater for themselves. There are worse things.

* * * * *

Eventually our Market adventures came to an end. In Winter those cold, bare flagstones struck a chill to your limbs. Kit's lifeless leg developed painful ulcers one year and she went through a bad winter, rocking back and forth in pain during the night watches. It seemed mean, somehow, to go off to sleep when somebody alongside you was in such misery. Some nights I stole across to the window to see if the lamplighter had been round to snuff out the gas jets of the street lights with his long pole. This was the welcome signal that morning was not far away. Nothing ever seemed so bad in the daylight, as most folk will agree.

Since nobody seemed able to cure this condition, some discussion ensued as to whether Kit should part with the limb. We were both relieved when the surgeon pronounced against it, because Kit would not have enough power to swing an artificial one. Kit was thankful at not having to make the drastic choice. She and I agreed it was best to stay in one piece if you could, and come Spring we found ourselves free to take it easy on Saturdays. We had opted for early retirement.

Fortunately, before Great Aunt Emily could come again with fresh ideas on propelling Kit into the rat race, Kit was discovered to have sufficient talent for piano playing to teach others. She was able to look the whole working world in the eye with the aid of a Five Finger Exercise Book and a metronome. Moreover, the entry into the musical world brought her to pastures new. She was drafted into the Primitive Methodist Choir. A whole new way of life opened up for her, and I got some side benefits as a privileged onlooker.

The Methodists appeared to be an amiable crowd and I secretly envied their ability to mix religion with entertainment. My Gospel Hall connection, even with Sunday School prize-givings, did not seem to feature songs and recitations in lighter vein (at least in the nineteen twenties) than:

> I should like to die, said Willie,
> If my Papa could die too.

Kit's new church was not averse to a bit of dancing and a spot of nonsense in their choir concerts and bazaars, and Kit's initiation came with an invitation to preside over the Flower Stall of the Bazaar which preceded the next Choir Concert.

The honour was to be shared with her friend Elsie, and

the main challenge was to decide what to wear, because your costume had to be appropriate to your wares and also to your concert item to follow in the evening. Your ingenuity in carrying out this link-up would be rewarded with a prize, and thus spurred on, the two girls put their heads together. Grandmother, despite a professed disdain for the Methodists' roundabout way of fundraising and rather frequent appeals, rose to the occasion.

'But I still don't see the sense in it,' she observed, handing down a goodly supply of her home made jams and pickles from the top shelf of the storecupboard. 'The same people give, and buy back again. Why don't they give the money in the first place?' It was as well she did not manage to discourage the Methodists by her logic. We should have missed a lot of fun. The necklace you never really wanted for your birthday might be just the thing for Mrs Brown's new two-piece. And Mr Brown's discarded Long Johns might be just the job for anybody with a mind to explore the Arctic.

We got the feeling that Grandmother was not half as reluctant as she made out, and she wanted Kit to look nice. She knew how important this was to her, and took Kit off to find the right equipment – a new floral dress 'off the peg' (no nonsense with the Singer Drophead!) from Lamb's big dress shop adjoining the Market, and a large, becoming picture hat with a white rose at the side, from Ethel's hat stall. I was amazed at Grandmother's generosity – the hat alone cost eighteen shillings and elevenpence halfpenny!

But she did look fine on The Day. We were very proud of her. Elsie's dress was somewhat plainer in colour and design, but made up for by the chaplet of flowers surrounding the brim of her round straw hat. Soon the hand-sewn aprons, embroidered traycloths, home made cakes and preserves, etc., found new homes. Just occasionally a person bought back the goods he or she had bequeathed. But even that had a certain logic about it, as Grandmother, most practical of all people, must have agreed. If you had bought a toby jug in Llandudno ten years ago for one and sixpence, there must have been something about it that took your fancy. And languishing on the White Elephant Stall, reduced to threepence, it *had* to be a bargain and deserved restoring to your china cabinet.

As the posies and plants on the Flower Stall were

snapped up, and people were doing justice to the strawberry cream teas, it was time for the tenors, baritones and basses to get to work, clear the trestle tables and rearrange the seating to face the brightly lit platform. The Choir Concert (the first it had been my privilege to encounter, and in retrospect the most impressive) got under way. Anxious as I was to applaud it all, for Kit's sake, I found myself struggling a little with my conscience to reconcile some of the items with Chapel life, even though we were seated in the Schoolroom which had been glorified for the occasion.

It was not so much the Stanley Holloway character reciting 'Albert And The Lion' in a very passable Lancashire dialect, which jolted me, as the huge fellow who possessed a deep bass voice and a pair of eyes that rolled in his head like giant marbles, for his costume included a black tunic or cloak, a pair of horns and a toasting fork. His song, to the best of my recollection, was a rendering of the words of the terrifying Apollyon out of Pilgrim's Progress. After the initial shock, I fell to wondering how his costume could possibly have related to the afternoon bazaar goods! The mind boggled. Did he sell firewood? Or crumpets?

Following a round of repartee and funny stories from two other men, there appeared a baritone on the stage who rendered, with great gusto, the tale of a man's unhappy choice of a second wife. The verses, one by one, recounted his mounting disaffection with her and each ended with the emphatic assertion, rendered as though every note was his last:

And I longed for the old 'un agen!

Kit and I might have politely joined in the thunderous applause if we had not been acutely aware that the performer's wife lay at that very moment ill in her bed at home, afflicted with a malady which threatened to be fatal.

'How *can* he?' muttered Kit, aghast, for the sick wife was Elsie's sister, and we stubbornly kept our hands pressed together. Maybe we were too hard on him. This could be his way of keeping cheerful. Certainly the weeks ahead were to be overshadowed.

Eventually it was Elsie's turn to mount the platform and to render in light, sweet soprano a cheerful little song which faithfully echoed her role of the afternoon...

Happy children... in the woods...
Gathering flowers... one by one...

each verse concluding:

Happy time... O happy time of youth

Kit's own contribution which followed, was not only appropriate to her costume and stallholding, but also to the occasion and the setting. Grandmother and I were entirely satisfied. Standing before the piano, a gilded basket of blooms at her feet, Kit went through her touching ballad about a London flowerseller, without a hitch. Each verse elaborated on the meagre lot of the damsel in the gutters of the East End and - lest we took refuge from our consciences in the thought that this was long ago and far away - each verse was followed by the plaintive chorus:

There are many... Sad and weary...
In this pleasant land of ours,
Crying ev'ry night so dreary:
'Won't you buy my pretty flow'rs?'

Fifty years later, I stand by my assertion that Kit's was far and away the best item in the programme. The sweet melancholy of her song appealed to me, even in my own 'happy time of youth', as being of star quality. I am sure the Methodists thought so. See how their social conscience has developed over the years!

So Kit's teens merged into her twenties, not without activity. Yet her role as a 'good spectator' also yielded dividends. She caught her family's enthusiasm for County Cricket. Uncle Sidney and my father, her two elder brothers, being businessmen, could adjust their working hours to suit the fixtures. In fact my mother, left to mind the shop on sunny summer days, voiced her suspicion that my father's surrender of his 'safe' job with the County Health Authorities was largely influenced by the activities on that field.

But this asset to our city was considerable. The battle for the Ashes with Australia always began on our ground, described as the most beautiful in England, and Kit enjoyed many happy hours in the Ladies' Pavilion.

The river bank, the foursquare tower and ancient grey stone of the Cathedral, plus St Andrew's Spire pointing unerringly to the blue heavens above, all made a beautiful backdrop for the nimble white figures on the green turf, and somehow combined to promote a reasonably hopeful view of mankind.

Worcester County Cricket Ground

CHAPTER 8

The Common Task

FAILING THE ELEVEN-PLUS is rather like dying without a decent burial. You scan the published lists in vain... a second time, even a third, and incredulously your name is not there, anywhere. It is as if, from the examiner's point of view, you had never been...

You may batter till Kingdom Come on the closed doors of Paradise (if you have set your sights so low as to equate the Girls' Grammar School thus) and never find out why, when or where you went wrong. All you will hear will be the distant imagined voice of the Examiner with his equivalent of 'Depart from me, for I never knew you.' It makes it so much worse if you *did* trim your lamp. Yours just wasn't bright enough.

Nor does it console you to find that the weeping, worrying candidate you tried to comfort during the examination lunch break is now being kitted out with her new uniform with the red piped edges to her blazer and a straw boater. *And* her tennis racquet and hockey stick, of course...

In a generous moment you may reflect how much worse it would have been for her because both her parents were teachers, but your only real refuge is to infer that you had not really fancied furthering your education with snobs (most of that school population being fee-paying) and that you never really tried to pass. Nobody believes you, but most people are too decent to say so. There are a few, a very few, who have the presence of mind to affect surprise at your situation. This may do something for your damaged ego and their hinted suspicion as to the fairness of the examiners will become a treasured memory.

So I had no alternative but to wend my way along the familiar route to the old, square red-bricked 'British' Girls' School in Clapgate that Autumn. I say 'wend', but the more appropriate word would be 'pound', for I rarely set out in time to arrive before the first stroke of the Cathedral clock chimed out. In fact that was usually my signal to break into a run, and with a clear path before me I might sprint across the threshold before the last stroke of nine.

On that first day of term I was met by an accusing voice from the top of the stone staircase as I stumbled upwards: 'You're late! And the headmistress is asking for you. She wanted to see you before school. It's too late now. Time for Assembly!' The teacher hurried on.

I reached the top landing, breathless, flung my plain blue blazer inside the cloakroom and tried to slip in unnoticed. We did not boast an assembly hall as such, but the folding glass screens which separated the three top classrooms were thrust back by the biggest and strongest of our kind, and the Presence on the headmistress's dais added sufficient lustre to command our subdued attention.

Miss Freeman was small and quite thin, but upright as a ramrod. Hair which might have been pretty left to its own devices was tightly folded and fastened to the crown of her head. Her skin was parchment-like in texture, her mouth firm and uncompromising. When she needed to scrutinize anything or anybody, she lifted the pince-nez which dangled on a fine chain from her left shoulder to the bridge of her small, straight nose. Her grey eyes, thus veiled, met mine briefly as I passed near her platform. She answered my unspoken query with an imperative gesture toward the ranks of girls in an assortment of summer prints. We did not boast a uniform.

Miss Griffiths was at the piano near the dais awaiting Miss Freeman's signal. Then the poised fingers leaped over the keyboard, slowed at the end of the introductory line and sharply struck 'the note' of our morning hymn. A hundred and fifty trebles swept into our shrill version of:

> New ev'ry morning is the love
> Our wakening and uprising prove...

It was so familiar that it was not necessary to concentrate on the small print. You could mouth the words fairly convincingly while your mind soared outwards beyond the narrow windows and the corner of the iron fire escape that was just visible at the farthest point. For a few more moments you were free from the pressures of this new school day with its fresh anxieties involved with 'moving up', its fevers and its failures. As the hymn tailed off to a dispiriting close, I felt it did little to inspire our hopes or stimulate our ambitions:

> The daily round, the common task,
> Will furnish all we need to ask –
> Room to deny ourselves; a road
> To bring us daily nearer God.

Room to deny ourselves? Oh no! Most of us, given the ghost of a chance, would ask much, much more than that.

Perhaps it was my apprehension as to Miss Freeman's undisclosed requirements of me that settled like a wet blanket upon my shoulders and brought to mind the long succession of morning assemblies just like this. In such a setting, religion and duty stood like two implacable sentries. Now came the Scripture reading from the fifth chapter of St Matthew and I gave it my attention unwillingly. For weeks in the previous term we had laboured over The Beatitudes as our teacher called them – learning them 'by heart'. O God, I thought in sudden panic, there had been little enough of learning and nothing at all of heart in it! Surely I would never in my life be able to recall those words with a spark of interest, let alone inspiration. We had stumbled through them, each in turn.

'Blessed are...' It was, surely, a long catalogue of unattainable virtues. 'Blessed are... the meek'. That was the worst one of all. Was it true that you could - and should - will yourself to be *meek?* The word stuck in my throat as shades of Uriah Heep flitted through my mind and nauseated me.

But it was Holy Writ. I ought never to feel like this! Then a hope pierced my gloom. Maybe it was the repetition that was so off-putting? The too frequent recitation of the words? But no! Other verses we had memorized in English literature class came alive to me. They set up a tune inside of you and your mind fell into step. What was that one about the tinker? I would never forget it, nor resent it:

> *I wish I were a pedlar man,*
> *With a horse to drive and a caravan;*
> *Where he comes from nobody knows -*
> *Or where he goes to - but on he goes!*

Anxious thoughts chased through my mind. There must be something wrong with me because I felt more affinity with the roving pedlar and his tinkling wares than with the Patient Man who sat on the mountainside telling people how to be good.

Now there was a scraping of feet and a communal sigh. Morning assembly was over, but Miss Freeman was holding up her hand for further attention before dismissal.

'This morning', she announced crisply, 'I want to draw your attention to the Roll of Honour' and indicated the framed document that hung on the wall behind her chair. I could see only faintly the half dozen names behind the glass and had no idea what they signified. Miss Freeman was continuing: 'It is seldom I can add a girl's name to this roll, but one of you gained one hundred percent marks in the end-of-year examinations last term. It is a rare event and I am adding her name to this list - Kathleen Lawrence! Thank you girls, you may now proceed to your classes for assessment this year.'

My morbid thoughts were swallowed up in surprise. Then disbelief. Surely nobody gave you full marks for *every* subject, on principle? Could Miss Freeman have contrived it somehow? But she wouldn't - not Miss Freeman. She wasn't like that. Anyway, why would she?

I cast my mind back over those exams and could recall

no flash of genius, no advent of a fairy godmother...
simply the silky smooth foolscap and the new shiny nib in
my pen. I had lifted the little lid off the inkwell and the
virginal whiteness of the blank sheets before me had
faintly excited me. But then – they always did. There
seemed something god-like about taking away your old,
dog-eared exercise books with their blots and corrected
errors, and presenting you, at the end of the Summer
Term with a fine, clean sheet on which to show what is in
you. I think I will not ask more in Heaven...

As we filed out and the 'monitresses' got to work
hauling the room dividers back into place, I received
congratulatory nudges from my immediate neighbour with
diffidence. I still doubted if I had truly qualified for the
Honours List, but if anybody then had equated that
feeling with 'meekness' I would have laughed in disbelief.
It was simply that I knew my own limitations.

For a few fleeting hours the 'daily round' had an aura
about it for me. With something akin to affection I watched
Mrs Patterson, our only married teacher, book in hand,
hovering restlessly around the classroom. After all, she
had defended me from Stella Jeffreys' contemptuous laugh
at Stratford-on-Avon when I had the apalling cheek to
perch on the edge of Shakespeare's chair for a second and
wish that I could put words together as he did. We were
on a school trip, and had covered the twenty five miles by
'bus to this fascinating Warwickshire town. 'Alright!
Alright!' she had said, touching my shoulder
encouragingly, 'There is no harm at all in hoping!' And
she had withered Stella Jeffreys with her sharp, bird-like
glare.

As now she darted from one school desk to the next,
startling the inept and the dreamers in turn, it seemed to
me that she got no great joy out of teaching, so perhaps
it was an over-rated profession, and failing the
eleven-plus was not the end of the world. But she had
much to cope with, apart from us. Kit had confided to me
that Mrs P. had married a Great War casualty, a
shell-shocked soldier, who gave her a difficult home life.
So she had need of all the beatitudes twice over!
Especially 'Blessed are the merciful'... for she could be
sharp!

Extending mercy to a person does not necessarily mean
you must have them on their knees before you. There are
more subtle demands upon forbearance in a school teacher,

and watching Mrs Patterson dealing with Dorothy Jones, it dawned upon me that I was unlikely to fulfil the needs of that profession anyway. When it was Dorothy's turn to recite, her hesitant memory, her weakness in the adenoidal region and her regrettable shortage of handkerchiefs required great self control on the part of both pupil and teacher. Mrs Patterson gave Dorothy her full attention without a visible quiver. At the conclusion of her 'piece' Dorothy slid thankfully to her seat. The teacher's head disappeared behind her own desk lid and seconds later, as she passed between the rows of children's desks, she slid towards Dorothy, with an admirable sleight of hand, one of those torn up squares of old sheeting with which she met such emergencies and silently passed on.

In mid-afternoon of that day Miss Freeman sent for me. On her desk was the Honours List, my name added in copper-plate handwriting. But there was more. In the year ahead a new school was in the making in our city which would provide a two year course of further education, mainly commercial, for thirteen-plus pupils, and though I was a year younger, she proposed to enter my name for the first entrance exam. To prepare for this she offered to move me up to her own (top) class, jumping the intermediate one, because I had suffered some handicap by not starting school until turned six years old. This, of course, must be why the pessimistic but successful entrant for that fatal scholarship examination had been in a class above me. It had puzzled me earlier.

It was true I had suffered a series of colds, chills and earaches in pre-school days and had landed up in the Ear, Nose and Throat ward. I scarcely remembered it, apart from the generous hypocrisy of the Nursing Sister. She had assured my father, when I was collected from the Infirmary, that I had been 'very brave' whereas I had howled most of the afternoon after they had left me there! It was not so much that I feared the operation (of course) but that they had told me they could not visit me while there because my mother would not be able to stand the sight of the red blankets on the hospital beds.

Why they did not admit that hospital rules forbade visitors to children's wards, I cannot think. The truth would have been more palatable. To be abandoned into the hands of people who were so heartless as to drape our beds with coverings indicative of the operating theatre was disconcerting. But I had been mollified when the Sister

despatched me home with full marks for valour, and had
no idea the delay would provide an educational drawback.

Now Miss Freeman proposed to 'take me in hand' and
recklessly I agreed to 'work very hard indeed'. It
appeared the next scholarship exam would be more than
usually competitive as the lists had been extended to
14-plus pupils who had not previously had the opportunity
to enter. 'There are only six free places,' warned the
headmistress. 'Ask your parents if they agree to your
entering, because it will mean extending your schooling by
one year or possibly two.'

As I turned to go, she gave me one of her rare, very
controlled smiles, and permission to leave school half an
hour earlier to mark my 'honours' and to tell my parents.
It meant I was free to go there and then. In order to
emphasize the effect of this privilege, I ran all the way
home and arrived in Friar Street breathless.

My mother was standing before the overmantel mirror,
waving her dark brown hair and curving the little fringe
on her forehead with metal curling tongues heated on the
bars of the open fire below. She was adopting the style of
the very popular Duchess of York (later to become our
Queen, and later still the 'Queen Mum').

I was forced to admit she was making a good job of it -
so much prettier than the tight 'bun' at the neck which
chapel folk favoured, and that it took careful concentration
not to scorch your ears and neck, but it was deflating
when she saw no significance in my early arrival. She
made no comment at all.

So my news became rather a damp squib, especially as
my father was not on hand, but it was duly digested in
time and agreed that I was to enter at the first
opportunity. There even seemed a faint prospect that I
might be 'paid for' if necessary. The fees were very small
compared with those of the Grammar Schools, for this was
to form part of the local Technical School complex.

So the year went on and when the lists were published
it took me some time to find my name. After the previous
fiasco I read the list from bottom upwards. I got third
place.

* * * * *

It was not an earth-shattering success, but it heralded
a much needed change of school scene. It was faintly

exhilarating to become part of a new set up in the City's educational programme which, for the first time, was introducing co-education.

Fortunately for Kit and me we had hitherto been able to repair our own lack of higher education by devouring the pages of The Gem and The Magnet, inherited from Kit's brothers at no outlay. They provided a mine of information, for how else could we have learned that scholarship boys fought off prejudice to become Football, Cricket or House Captains through sheer merit – or what thundering good chaps the aristocracy were once their eyes were opened to a fellow's true worth.

Moreover, when fully digested and thirsting for more, one could repair to Mrs Braithwaite (only three doors away) who was a secondhand bookseller and paperback exchanger. She would trade you one 'used' magazine for two of yours, which I now recognize to be entirely reasonable, though appearing a bit one-sided at the time.

But what a task it was to thumb through her pile, while she stood gravely by, always clad in her hat and coat for some reason, which was a bit disquieting. Could she be tiring of the rotund husband who somehow did not seem quite the right match for her? Was she poised for flight? Either way, you felt obliged to quicken your search for the magazine numbers which followed in sequence from your previous finds, otherwise you might never know what happened to the innocent boy who was suspected of thieving, cheating or having some skeleton in his cupboard which had baffled investigation in previous instalments.

However, in Kit's glass-fronted bookcase was a copy of 'The Channings' which could be read without such hazards. Though I cannot recall full details of the plot, it was written in the best school tale tradition by Mrs Henry Wood, a Worcester-born writer. Furthermore we discovered it was based on her personal knowledge of our King's School where the boys were quartered in the old dwellings built in the Cathedral grounds. Her five brothers all attended there. Her characters and their adventures added significantly to our sense of values and to our interest in the straw-hatted, striped-blazered young gentlemen who strolled or crocodiled along Friar Street and with whom we occasionally rubbed shoulders in Mrs Evans' sweet shop next door.

So I went along to inspect the little placque, in the north transept of the Cathedral, which commemorated the writer. Of even more interest was the one on the wall of Danesbury House, 18 Sidbury, and a mere stone's throw from where we were reading her stories. Not inappropriately it was a bookshop at this time in the charge of two dignified maiden sisters, the Misses Flood. This, of course, gave one the right to enter the premises and to savour the atmosphere of the site which had provided the childhood home of the writer, then Ellen Price.

Only two of Ellen's five sisters survived childhood, so this imaginative little girl would have witnessed the trauma of infant mortality which would provide an important part of her writings. No wonder she memorised Gray's 'Elegy' in its entirety!

'Is there something I can do for you, dear?' enquired the elder Miss Flood, slightly exasperated after I had peeked around their immaculate shelves for twenty minutes, and I had to confess that I was 'only looking'. But I promised to return when I had the wherewithal to make a purchase and assured them I thought a bookshop the most fascinating place there was. Which was not mere flattery – for the sight of those rows and rows of new, glossy, unopened volumes sends something akin to a thrill down my spine still. Each cover is like a closed door which may swing ajar and admit one instantly into a whole new world.

Danesbury House

So I made friends with the Misses Flood and they invited me to attend their Temperance Class with them for they were earnest members of the Band of Hope. Since Mrs Henry Wood had started on her road to fame by winning a prize from the Scottish Temperance League with her story 'Danesbury House', their link with her was firmly established. I fell in with their suggestion and went with them for a time to the temperance classes at the nearby

Welcome Mission in our own Friar Street, and willingly
signed the pledge.

Though we were privileged to read Mrs Wood's epics in
their completed form, it appeared she had begun as a
serial writer. Her readers were of a social class which
rendered them independent of Mrs Braithwaite's bargain
counter – yet their hazards were greater. Ellen (Mrs
Henry Wood, wife of banker and shipping merchant) fell ill
and the editor of the New Monthly Magazine scanned his
post anxiously at the news that each instalment might be
the last, leaving his readers with a permanent cliffhanger.

Then into this dignified, privileged, literary world came
a dramatic intervention which saved their day. A complete
stranger, a north country woman, sought out the writer
who then languished in Upper Norwood, South London,
seemingly incurable. How I would love to have been there,
for the scene strikes one as so improbable! The visitor in
the old poke bonnet somehow convinced the novelist that
the same healing power which had operated in the life of
Naaman, the distinguished but leprous Captain of the Host
of Syria in biblical days, could now be applied to the
writer's need.

Surprisingly, Mrs Wood allowed the unlikely handmaiden
of the Lord to minister to her the prayer of faith, and the
tide of her failing health was turned. 'East Lynne'
progressed unhindered to its affecting conclusion, telling
of faithless love, repentance and of wrongs forgiven. (One
hundred and twenty years later the TV version is meeting
with wide acclaim).

It was all very exciting, but talking to my Gospel Hall
Sunday School teacher about miracles I got a cautious
response, surprising in the Bible-believing Plymouth
Brethren. 'Most of these "signs" died out with the Early
Church,' she warned hesitantly, 'Except perhaps for
special cases...' and went on to point out that Bible
stories were 'for our learning,' to be applied spiritually.
This was disappointing. If the lively and dramatic parts
which so appealed to me were out of date, what of the rest
of it? And how did you define a special case? I knew if I
were ill very few ministering angels would take a hopeful
view of me.

Fortunately I was not feeling ill at that time and could
afford to shelve this disconcerting problem, never for a
moment suspecting that is would shortly become a
determining factor in my life.

I doubted if the Plymouth Brethren would regard a novelist as a 'special case' - but when you come to think of it, neither would the Israelis think a Captain of the Host of Syria was! Seemingly God had his own rules...

Suffice it to say that Mrs Wood, then in her late forties yet only on the threshold of her writing career, lived on for another twenty six years and wrote more than thirty books for an appreciative public. Michael Craze, local historian in the village of Whittington where the Woods were married, sums her up thus: 'She contrived an excellent plot, handled all her characters well, told a good tale and was healthily pious.' Her work was translated into every known language including Parsee and Hindustani so she made her own inimitable contribution to the welfare of the British Empire, as well as to me, and to the cause of true love.

So perhaps she *was* a special case. There are few greater delights in life than a 'good read.'

Mrs Henry Wood

Worcester Public Hall
circa 1928

CHAPTER 9

"Touching the Hem"

I WAS ALL OF twelve years old when the revivalist came to our city. He took the Public Hall for a month for a widely advertised Revival and Divine Healing Campaign. Studying the posters I considered this must be important, for that venue had previously provided a platform for Charles Dickens, the Swedish Nightingale Jenny Lind, Christabel Pankhurst and other such notables.

But it was Olga Evans's Uncle Bert who picqued my curiosity about Pastor Edward Jeffreys in the first place.

Entering the sweet shop with nothing more weighty on my mind than a couple of ounces of Jap Nuggets, I found Uncle Bert behind the counter with his hand in a jar of mint humbugs and an expression on his face which betokened deep introspection.

'I can't make up my mind about him,' he confessed to his only other customer at the time, a barber from a nearby shop.

If you are of a communicative turn of mind, as Uncle Bert was, you cannot do better than open a shop for there is bound to be the odd customer who will lend you his ears for a short time in the hope of getting good weight. Uncle Bert had found such a one, and whilst juggling the humbugs on the scales he seemed to be weighing Pastor Jeffreys up too. It appeared Uncle Bert had made his first appearance among the audience at the opening session on the previous evening.

'Well, what went on?' queried his listener, anxious for news rather than Uncle Bert's opinion, 'Were there any cures?'

'I think so,' responded Uncle Bert, 'There was a big crowd in front of the platform and I did see a few walking sticks and hearing aids – that sort of thing – left around. I mean to say... they'd have been taken home if the people hadn't been cured, wouldn't they?'

The barber was not so trusting. 'Might have been put there for effect,' he said, 'It's what goes on behind the scenes I like to know about. I bet he's in it for the money.'

Uncle Bert was reluctant to dismiss his night's adventure so tardily, or to admit to his own gullibility.

'He seems a nice chap,' he defended himself, 'I think he's genuine meself.'

'How does he do it then?' demanded the customer, 'If he really gets any cures, that is. Hypnotism, I shouldn't wonder.'

Uncle Bert shook his head, wonderingly. 'It didn't look like it – but there was that Dr Brodie who came on the music halls once – I wonder what he used? He seemed to be able to do some queer things.'

'Electrical gadgets of some sort,' averred the customer. 'Electric shocks can do marvellous things, I've heard. Even cure lunatics. Did it look as if they'd had electric shocks?'

'Well, no,' responded Uncle Bert, a little more

positively now. 'I think I should have known if it was that. I... I went out meself, you know, to be healed... that is.'

'You did!' ejaculated the customer, 'Whatever for? What you got wrong with you?'

Olga's Uncle Bert touched his glasses. 'It's for eyesight, as well, you know. There's no limit to what he can do - as long as you got faith. It's no good if you got no faith. Might as well stay at home.'

'You're still wearing your specs though,' pointed out the barber, 'Didn't you have the faith for it then? What went on?'

Uncle Bert was nonplussed at so direct a challenge. 'Well, I mean to say... I've got to see how it goes on, haven't I?'

'If you don't leave your specs off,' pointed out the customer, 'You won't know whether you're cured or not. In my opinion its all a lot of poppycock'; pocketing his mint humbugs, he departed.

Uncle Bert looked thoughtful as he attended to me. I asked if Olga was in, and as he put my coppers in the till he invited me to come into the room behind the shop to see if she wanted to play. Mrs Evans was sitting peacefully before the coal fire, resting until it was her turn to answer the shop bell. As she gave me her usual warm smile, Uncle Bert launched into his account of the recent conversation over the counter. 'He could be right, you know,' he informed his sister-in-law, 'Some of those people throw away their crutches and things, to show their faith!'

Before Mrs Evans could give her rather reluctant attention to the matter, for she had not been to the Public Hall for first-hand information, Uncle Bert snatched off his horn rims and tossed them into the fire!

'You fool, Bert!' shrieked Olga's mother in alarm, and with amazing dexterity for one who had only just been aroused from torpor, she snatched up the glasses before they tumbled from the top bar of her firegrate into the flames, and dropped them on to the thick hearthrug. She cradled her stinging fingers with an expression of mingled wrath and anguish.

Bert was at a loss for words. Snatching up the offending specs, he marched off rapidly into the scullery beyond, from where he did not emerge even when the shop bell tinkled. Mrs Evans sighed and took her turn, blowing on her fingers.

Without more ado I went off to tell my parents about it, for there is something very satisfying about being the bearer of news. They were discussing the same topic, considering whether it was advisable to persuade Kit to attend the divine healing campaign. They themselves had reservations about the high sounding publicity and newspaper reports. My account of Bert Evans' reaction did little to encourage them.

They were not against evangelists, as such, Mother pointed out. In fact she paid tribute to one who, from the Gospel Hall platform, had made her understand far more clearly what the Gospel was all about than had her respectable Anglican upbringing by her godly mother. All the same, she and my father felt there were things here even the Gospel Hall would question.

But it so happened, for reasons not disclosed to their offspring, that they had not attended the Gospel Hall so much of late. We might not have noticed, but for Mother's newstyle hairdo and the furry opera cloak she had mysteriously acquired with which to accompany Kit somewhere. Then when they went to see 'East Lynne' at the Arcade Cinema, I did wonder if our scene was changing. But after all, they might well think it justifiable to support a Worcester-born authoress; the theme was about a repentant sinner, and it featured a woman who managed to penetrate an august household to become nurse to her own child (which had a biblical precedent in the story of Moses). Then came the *Sunday* afternoon when our West Bromwich cousins came to visit at Grandmother's and we were allowed to go with them to Uncle Bert's next door and buy ice cream! Oh the guilt of that first Sunday lick!

But when somebody hinted that Kit and Mother had gone to the Theatre Royal where 'The Mikado' was being performed, I thought it highly unlikely, particularly when I heard snatches of the songs in Grandmother's parlour. The same words repeated over and over again! As if they had not been understood at first! Such a waste of time when they could be getting on with the story, whatever it was. Surely nobody, least of all our mother, would succumb to the wiles of the world, the flesh and the devil for that! It was very odd.

Before I could reach any firm conclusion, the revivalist came. Every evening long queues filled the Cornmarket –

the big open square in front of the Public Hall - and surrounded the building on all sides waiting for the doors to open at 7 o'clock. Interest mounted and after the initial hesitation it was decided that Kit ought to go. Mother would never have forgiven herself if she had been a party to passing over what might be the chance of a lifetime for Kit, now in her early twenties. Such an important time in one's life, Mother pointed out.

The family was reluctant for Kit to feel she was being made a spectacle of, and it took a good deal of heartsearching to decide whether they had the right kind of 'faith' for this sort of thing. Putting that to the test can be quite an unnerving experience to a sensitive soul (maybe Kit and Mother had 'The Mikado' on their consciences) but eventually courage was summoned and I got into a turmoil of expectation, particularly on the night before we were to take Kit to the Public Hall.

We really were in earnest in our prayers that night. There had been times when Naomi and I had said our prayers together and had the curious sensation of breaking into laughter half way through. I have yet to discover if this is unique, or which of us caused it, so we devised a system whereby we set aside a few moments before starting prayers to have our 'laugh out', as we called it, and summoned all the mirth we could in an effort to get it out of our system. I don't think it always worked.

But I clearly recalled the urgent persuasion with which I assailed the courts of Heaven on Kit's behalf. Wildly I promised God all kinds of things if only He would put Kit right so that she walked like the rest of us. The life I pledged myself to lead henceforth and forever was probably beyond the capacity of the noblest of saints, but not being acquainted with saints I did not know it then. I meant every syllable.

It really is not so odd as it now sounds to try to bargain with the Almighty, for the story of Jacob at the foot of the ladder is one of the first Bible episodes a child hears and becomes familiar with. Lying on his back with nothing but a stone for a pillow, and in a predicament of his own making, he had less to offer than I had, it seemed to me, when he 'vowed a vow' at Bethel. In exchange for a few trifles like the constant protection of the Almighty, enough to eat, enough to wear and the chance of reconciliation with the family he had wronged, Jacob generously offered 'The Lord shall be my God.'

I have since heard of the phrase 'sanctified commensense'. In my city of Worcester, one is prompted to substitute 'sanctified sauce' as a more apt description. Yet he came out of it all pretty well, as any student of the Book of Genesis will tell you. And if the history – the strange, stubborn, chequered history of that nation which sprang from his loins – is anything to go by, God is very good about keeping bargains even when He does not seem to get very much out of them.

* * * * *

'I know a way in, through a side door,' said Connie Robbins during afternoon break on the following day, 'If we go straight up there after school, we can get in and see the last half hour.'

Connie's conspiratorial air whetted my appetite to get a preview of the campaign meetings at the end of the afternoon 'healing session' which attracted the sick and the afflicted who could not queue up in the evenings. So we took the Clapgate route home and crept into the hall unobserved to see if any miracles were taking place.

Our mood of excited curiosity became subdued as soon as we entered. Considering the stir caused by the posters splashed around our locality, the atmosphere seemed remarkably hushed at four o'clock in the afternoon. With the huge pipe organ playing softly in the background, the crowd was singing gently:

> *She only touched the hem of his garment*
> *As to his side she stole,*
> *Amid the crowd that hovered around him –*
> *And straightway she was whole!*

I recognized, with some surprise, the old Biblical story of the woman afflicted with 'an issue of blood' for eighteen years without relief. I had never quite liked her story in Sunday School because her long years of suffering *and* reducing herself to beggary through doctor's bills seemed painful to contemplate. Yet this gentle song gave the episode new appeal. It seemed that the purpose of this gathering was to prove that the age of miracles had not passed and that the revelation had a personal application for each verse of the printed song concluded:

O touch the hem of his garment
And thou, too, shalt be free;
His saving power this very hour
Shall bring new life to thee

'His saving power...' 'His saving power...' The refrain seemed to emphasize the spiritual rather than the physical application, as did the preaching of the evangelist, I noted. Disappointed at first, yet strangely reassured, I listened on. Perhaps this strange assembly was not so very different from the familiar Gospel Hall?

The discourse finished, the preacher came down from the platform to confer with a group of people in the space in front of the audience but we were too far away to know very much of what went on, and knowing we were to be there that evening I agreed when Connie felt the need to depart and see what her mother had for tea. They were a large family, so her concern was understandable.

In the evening the hall was very full. We were packed like sardines in a row near the back of the gallery. Kit was way down in front on the ground floor with my mother to sponsor her. It was probably my mother's own involvement which had tipped the scales in persuading Kit to come. Mother suffered from something called an 'inguinal hernia' for which her doctor had prescribed an appliance, though I doubt if she would have made it known except in the present circumstances. She offered to join Kit in the 'healing row' when the time came, largely because of her tremendous affection and concern for Kit which seemed greater than normally existed between sisters-in-law. I believe Mother wanted nothing more from life then than to see Kit well and happily married, for she knew Kit was capable of warm affection which ought not to be wasted.

The auditorium was a hive of activity for some time after we were admitted. Stewards were marshalling latecomers into the odd vacant seats here and there. A subdued buzz of conversation added to the sense of expectancy. Grandmother and I looked around us and spotted many neighbours and acquaintances. Olga Evans' Uncle Bert was just visible, sitting against the gangway on the ground floor. Though I felt a pang of disappointment at seeing his horn-rimmed specs; they seemed from that distance to be none the worse for their adventure, which was something to be thankful for. I could not glimpse any other members of his family, but concluded they must have been co-operative in releasing him from the shop early. He must have got in the queue in good time to get such a good seat.

A hush descended on the crowd as the platform party emerged from doors at the back of the big platform and took their seats. Over and above them, draped across the organ pipes, was a large white banner which proclaimed in red and blue poster paint:

JESUS CHRIST
THE SAME YESTERDAY AND TODAY AND FOREVER!

The instrumentalists who had been feeling their way along their keyboards, arranging music sheets and conferring with each other, now settled in readiness. A slim, good looking young man rose smartly to his feet and greeted the audience with a wide smile and a few words of welcome before announcing the first song on the printed sheet which had been issued to us. The singing was lively, quick and enthusiastic in response to the movements of the young conductor, who brought the proceedings to a satisfactory momentum when he had them singing, over and over again, the chorus to one of the revival songs. It was an obvious favourite:

In the sweet bye and bye...
In the sweet bye and bye
I have a mansion so bright and so fair –
Won't it be lovely when we get there...

and even I, who had never settled my secret worry about where God would put us all when we reached the Promised Land, was caught up in its joyful, liberating tempo. Some were even waving handkerchiefs to emphasize their anticipation. I did not feel I could manage that... I stole a sideways glance at Grandmother and found she was dangling hers rather ineffectively at half mast. Then I realized, with some relief, that I did not have with me a handkerchief in the right state for public display, and hoped the Lord would not take this as a sign of defection after all my pledges of the night before.

'Just once more,' urged the song-leader, 'before Pastor Jeffreys brings to you the Gospel message for tonight,' and he swept his long arms into an encouraging movement. I studied the photograph on the front of our song sheet.

Pastor Edward Jeffreys was the founder of a new revival movement called The Bethel Evangelistic Society. He had come from Bristol, the venue of his first successful campaign, and was now advancing into the Midlands. We had heard he was the son of a Welsh miner-turned-preacher, the winsome, silver-haired Stephen Jeffreys, who had become involved in evangelism as a result of the Welsh Revival at the turn of the century. Edward, the son, appeared to be an attractive man in his early thirties. I liked the movement of his well-brushed shapely head and the almost modest way in which at times he rested his brow upon his right hand and was lost to our view momentarily.

Then he rose to his feet, Bible in hand, and though we were so far from the platform it seemed that his thoughtful, deep-set eyes penetrated even to the back of the gallery as he emphasized his point. This appeared to be that though Christ died for all, it depended upon the individual response to that sacrifice whether it became effective for us, or not. He took a text from one of St Paul's letters - the one to the Ephesians - 'And *you* hath He quickened, who were dead in trespasses and sins!' With a pointing finger, moving in turn in all directions, he repeated the text and involved us all in his final appeal for personal, individual response, leaving us in no doubt as to the urgent necessity for doing so.

'It doesn't matter what your background, your church connection or your upbringing,' he added, 'This is *your* time to come to Christ! Your moment of decision!' He invited the members of the audience to signify assent by rising momentarily to their feet. I searched my heart anxiously. With all my upbringing and the influence of the Gospel Hall Sunday School, I could not recall that I had ever consciously made such a choice. He was counting converts and rallying stragglers, and failed to see my momentary stand so I did not add to the tally that night. As I slid back to my seat, Grandmother pressed my arm. I blushed. So she had seen. And the preacher had asked for 'every eye to be closed.' No matter. The die was cast now. Perhaps it was not a bad thing to have a witness, especially if you were too small for the preacher to see!

It was not perhaps a dramatic or touching conversion, but I know now that of all the transactions I have made subsequently, none has been more valid or less regretted than this one. Bizarre and theatrical though it may seem, impure as may have been my motives, I experienced a sense of exhilaration, relief and wellbeing that comes to us all too seldom in life.

Later we struggled to join Kit and Mother down below. There was a lot of movement now, as the sick people moved, a group at a time, to the area reserved for them. Pastor Jeffreys left the platform to join the stream of supplicants and I saw how faithfully his photograph had represented him. The thoughtful, challenging eyes were kind now and very, very concerned as he moved from one person to the next for the moment of entreaty and prayer. Now and again he paused to confer with the 'patient', lifting a hand or finger before the eyes of the blind or poorsighted, testing the reactions of the deaf, moving exploratory fingers over wasted limbs. The atmosphere was surprisingly controlled for so motley and curious a crowd. The sense of human need seemed to transcend all other emotions and to nullify the accusations of selfish motives which had been raised.

Now and again, when some sign of 'success' or response to the prayer was shown by some encouraging sign or movement, an involuntary murmur of relief or delight escaped the watching people, and the chorus of encouragement and supplication was continued gently and earnestly:

Jesus is passing this way... ay...
Is passing this way... today...

Then it was Mother and Kit's turn for the 'laying on of hands'. The preacher's thoughtful, grey eyes encountered Kit's troubled ones. The iron caliper had been removed and laid on the ground beside her. Since she could not stand without it, she remained on the front row of seats. The Pastor bent forward to ask the nature of her trouble and how long she had been so affected. After my mother made the necessary response, he laid his gentle, capable hands upon Kit's head and right shoulder. As I glimpsed her dark, glossy hair beneath his curving fingers, I felt a sharp constriction in my throat and chest. I wanted to cry, without in the least knowing why.

There was no jargon or formula. After a second or two of silence, he began to pray, quietly at first, then increasing in urgency. As the voice ceased, we opened our eyes in the silence. The Pastor spoke to Kit in an undertone. She swallowed hard and moved towards the edge of the chair so that the little, helpless limb might touch the ground. Instinctively she groped for assistance, and just as instinctively my mother offered it, then hesitated, her eloquent eyes questioning and compassionate.

Kit made an attempt to rise without help. Somehow the strength so longed for did not come... Supported on either side she took one or two steps. Still the desired vigour failed to appear in the heavy, relaxed limb. The Pastor continued with her for a while longer, then encouraged her to continue to pray, to trust and to return if need be. 'God *can* do it,' he stressed, the lines of compassion around his eyes deepening. 'We are all in His hands...'

Hardly knowing what to say, we helped Kit away from the noisy, dispersing crowd and bore her down the quiet streets to home. We were no longer exhilarated, but some stubborn hope persisted. Back in the Friar Street living room Kit removed her caliper and surgical boot for the night, as was her custom at the fireside. She lifted the lifeless limb and laid it across her other knee, stroking it with questioning fingers. For Kit, so far, no miracle...

'I don't care,' I thought wildly, 'I don't care if it takes days or weeks or months... but let it come some time!'

It was almost an anticlimax next morning to learn that my mother had, in fact, received her own healing! The truss was discarded.

Quite honestly, I didn't know whether to laugh or cry. I don't think any of us did.

But Kit was very good about it. And we never seriously regretted that day's adventures.

Canal boats today at Lowesmoor Wharf

CHAPTER 10

Successors to the Boat People

NOBODY IS SUPPOSED to look a gift horse in the mouth, least of all a revival preacher without fixed income or financial backing. But Pastor Jeffreys must have raised a quizzical eyebrow when offered possession of Lowesmoor Chapel when his campaign drew to a close.

The Chapel had been built in 1823 when the waterways of England provided major traffic routes. Worcester was a thriving inland port and the nearby canal established Lowesmoor as the City Centre, thronged by day by an army of dock labourers. By night the men of the barges tied up their vessels at the canal banks and looked for congenial company. Pubs, clubs, hotels and music halls sprang up. Here Worcester-born Vesta Tilley took her first lithesome steps to fame, and a stage was set for the young Edward Elgar to emerge into his world of harmony as conductor of a theatre orchestra.

It was Susanna Knapp who saw Lowesmoor as a Mission Field in 1822 - that man could not live by entertainment alone - and persuaded her brother John to sell her a piece of land opposite the wharf for £250 'with a view to the erection of a chapel for religious worship, especially for the Boat People.' Legal jargon adds sober emphasis to its directives, so one may not be entirely justified in the suspicion that Brother John did not share his sister's laudable sentiments. The spidery handwriting of the Conveyance of the 'parcel of land' continues across parchment nearly 3 feet wide, '...and will warrant by these presents to be peaceably and quietly held and enjoyed without any let, suit, social eviction, or interruption by the said John Knapp, his heirs or assignees...'

Soon rousing Wesley hymns rose to compete with popular songs, touching ballads and the tapping of dancing feet across the road at The Alhambra. In view of river craft being at the mercy of heavy drinkers and (possibly) brother John's interventions, the popular, hearty composition of Charles Wesley would be enjoyed:

And are we yet alive, And see each other's face?
Glory and praise to Jesus give, For His
redeeming grace!

But by one adroit sleight of hand the nearby Great Western Railway ruined fifty years of prosperity in Lowesmoor. They purchased a controlling interest in the waterways and suppressed canal traffic. The whole area fell into decline and when the bluff bargees came no more from the canal banks to raise their hearty voices in praise, it seemed that the chapel lost heart also. The few remaining worshippers clung on with stubborn loyalty, but there is something dispiriting about singing 'The gates of hell shall never 'gainst His church prevail' when you are surrounded by rows and rows of empty pews - especially if they are overtaken by dry rot and woodworm, for here you have enemies to whose better nature you can never appeal. 'Change and decay in all around I see' might well have been the chapel's swan song.

It may be that the Lowesmoor area will not come again into its own until waterways are re-recognized for their value in the world of transport, and Worcester regains its status as an inland port. That day may yet come - but for Lowesmoor Chapel more immediate reinforcements were at hand in 1928. The little party of chapel members who attended the Divine Healing Campaign, together with a couple of hundred other Worcester citizens, put their faith into action and turned the old trustees' decaying responsibility into a lively, thriving community. The chapel became the second church of the Bethel Evangelistic Society, whilst its founding pastor moved on into the Black Country, the Potteries and the 'dark satanic mills' of the north of England.

So the church was cleaned, repaired and restored. The long neglected gallery was reopened, the pillars strengthened and a new membership enrolled. Though to many of the Public Hall audience which had queued around the building night after night the Campaign had been a flash in the pan, perhaps a fading vision, others were reluctant to see the end of their spiritual adventure. Many had received a life-changing experience. Kit, showing an independence of spirit which ought to have been admired, but probably was not, decided to stick with the Primitive Methodists. But my immediate family (including the toddlers of course) went a good way towards filling one of the high backed central pews of 'Bethel.' Our family life took a new turn, and if I had feared it would prove a restricting one, I was wrong.

My father overcame his initial caution (about joining) because he took so well to the tall, dark young man who had been the Campaign song leader and who now became pastor. They discovered they shared the same birthday date, though I think our new pastor was less influenced by that than by my father's drollery and by his church and business experience when he invited Father to become church secretary.

My mother, despite the multitude of chores which filled her days, found time to enjoy life in this new setting. She was still in her mid-thirties, my father three or four years

older, and as soon as things began to look up
business-wise, we moved to a new home a couple of miles
from the shop. This soon became open house for many
young Bethelites who especially valued Mother's friendship.
Even after five babies, her figure was trim, she had a
quick and lively walk, and was keenly interested in the
youngsters' ups and downs.

* * * * *

It was as well we made so many friends, for our new
way of life formed something of a barrier between us and
our relatives. Neither the Hardwicks nor the Lawrences
welcomed hot gospelling, but bore patiently with us in the
hope that it would not last over long or be brought to
their notice too often. Mother had been born midway
between Aunt Alice and Aunt Trudie and the three of them
had been quite close, particularly as their offspring were
roughly in the same age group.

Aunt Trudie was the most outspoken. 'Our Kate must
be mad!' she said, referring to my mother, 'Fancy getting
mixed up with that lot!' For Trudie

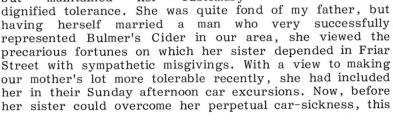

their mother's example and Anglican
upbringing more than sufficed. She
maintained her links with St
Nicholas', Worcester's most central
church, where Frances Ridley
Havergal's father had once been
rector, and Trudie kept it all in
perspective. She had thought it bad
enough when my mother defected to
the Gospel Hall and got 'saved'
there, but since that had occurred
as a result of my father's pursuit of
her, it was more understandable...

Aunt Alice was inclined to agree
but maintained her customary
dignified tolerance. She was quite fond of my father, but
having herself married a man who very successfully
represented Bulmer's Cider in our area, she viewed the
precarious fortunes on which her sister depended in Friar
Street with sympathetic misgivings. With a view to making
our mother's lot more tolerable recently, she had included
her in their Sunday afternoon car excursions. Now, before
her sister could overcome her perpetual car-sickness, this

new religious diversion had taken her out of Alice's sphere of benevolence. Perhaps it was as well. It is not conducive to the enjoyment of other travellers when one passenger turns a funny colour and either the car must be halted miles from its destination, or worse consequences follow. For my mother it was a happy release from her predicament; she was never quite convinced by Alice that motoring was a thing you got used to... *if* you tried!

The Lawrence side were more lighthearted about it. My grandfather had been a founder member of the Plymouth Brethren assembly in Worcester, and later became caretaker of the Welcome Mission, so he thought he had seen it all before. Uncle Sidney and Uncle Walter teased Naomi and me with their wine glasses and pronounced themselves our 'wicked uncles'. Uncle Reg was too busy building up his nice home and bringing up his auburn-haired daughter to take much notice, while Harry (the youngest and so near our own age that we dispensed with his title) was enjoying his motoring career and secondary role as drummer of a dance band. But we were fond of them all and kept alive our hopes for their enlightenment in due time.

Presumably other families were similarly affected. For younger Bethelites still living under parental roofs, the situation was awkward. Such parents regarded the sudden urge for churchgoing as sheer perversity in their young, or that they had contracted religious mania. Lack of sympathy in their own homes drove some of these younger folk into ours. They enjoyed my father's easy badinage and my mother's warm interest in them. For me it was a fascinating exploration into other people's lives.

The Book of Deuteronomy and the plight of the Gadarene swine had combined to raise a question mark in the mind of one student teacher as to the wisdom of eating pork. She was despatched to teach in a village school and found herself in lodgings, her menu at the mercy of a landlady. Landladies were hard to come by in Badsey, so she confided in my mother in the lovely, well modulated voice which was her outstanding feature.

On her first day in 'digs' she encountered nothing more problematical than tomatoes served with *sugar*, but on the second day, sure enough, the breakfast table boasted a poached egg and a curling rasher. 'So while I was saying 'grace', explained Dorothy, 'I asked the Lord to make it taste really nasty if I ought not to eat it.'

'And what happened,' asked Mother, with vested interest for we were bacon eaters too when it was available.

'I never tasted better,' Dorothy concluded simply.

'What a mercy, dear,' responded Mother in relief, 'You're thin as a rake already! But I'm sure you did right to ask.'

An attractive, brown-eyed nurse often made our home her rendezvous between duties. The young pastor was falling rapidly in love with her but she was being hard-to-get. She could afford to. She was quite lovely, in and out of uniform. This time it was the young minister who came to confide in my mother. The light of his life had just come out in a new Spring outfit.

'She looked marvellous,' he declared, 'This coat... a sort of fancy tweed... it had a blaze bottom.'

Soon we saw it for ourselves and found that Mother had rightly interpreted this as a flared skirt. Fortunately his vocabulary in the pulpit was more reliable.

One of a quartet of inseparables (christened by my father The Four Bright Sparks) had the misfortune to ladder her only decent pair of stockings as she dressed for church one Sunday morning. She succumbed to temptation and popped up to the corner shop, opened for newspapers. Her friends were dubious about the remedy, and the debate continued as they fell in with us on the way to church.

'Honestly, Mrs Lawrence,' she assured my mother, 'How could I do anything else? My last pair it was! It must have been the Devil! I mean to say, you can't go to Communion in laddered stockings, can you?'

The general opinion was that you could, and that the Lord would be better pleased by that than by your patronising the vendors of Sunday newspapers. But Bertha was not truly convinced and it was not a matter over which you could easily quote chapter and verse.

As we settled into our pew I found time to glance around curiously at the crowd which was filing in from all directions. Away to the left was the little man with round steel-rimmed spectacles who rejoiced so much over his healing, but even more that his sins had been forgiven, though you would not have judged him likely to harbour much guilt. He had such a pleasant demeanor. But you never can tell. In some moment of aberration my father failed to recall his name and described him to us vaguely

as 'You know - the "blotted out" fellow.' And we did
know, of course. It was Mr Redding. Every time he had
the chance he would request the chorus:

> *God has blotted them out; God has blotted them out.*
> *My sins, like a cloud, hung over me.*
> *He blotted them out when He set me free...*

I felt there was probably many a man whose guilt was
heavier, yet whose sense of relief was less. Perhaps, just
as we differ in our 'pain thresholds' so we do in our guilt
thresholds. I seemed to recall from somewhere the words,
'They who feign would serve Thee best are conscious most
of wrong within.' It really was odd - but I had a lifetime
ahead of me in which to sort it out...

In the pew beside us was the pretty, dainty woman
whose skin had become tinged with a pale violet hue after
she had been (I understood) overdosed or wrongly treated
with some drug in hospital. In any other circumstances
this would have been a charming shade, but quite
naturally all this quiet woman wanted was to conform to
the society around her. The medical people could not cure
her, so she sought divine aid. Some there were who
thought they detected a gradual lightning of her colour,
but I eventually concluded this was due to the lovely smile
which lit up her features. All our goodwill flowed out to
her.

Here under this glass-domed roof the people came
together, the strong and the weak, the healed and the
hopeful, the privileged and the odd ones, brought into a
common bond by this new affection. Soon we were singing
with more than a hundred others the pre-Communion
hymn:

> *Break Thou the bread of life, Dear Lord to me,*
> *As Thou didst break the loaves beside the sea;*
> *Beyond the sacred page, I seek Thee Lord,*
> *My spirit pants for Thee, O Living Word...*

Incredibly, miraculously, the motley crowd had been
marshalled into a unanimity of heart and purpose that had
to be shared to be believed. Sincerity hovered like a
modest dove over the bowed heads as the stewards moved
quietly among the people with the wafer bread and the
Communion wine.

Bethel preachers were apt to throw up barriers with other denominations by disdaining rites and ceremonies, but there was one, proclaimed our pastor, which was different. It was fundamental. It was in the Word. He gave us chapter and verse, and convinced us that baptism was not an optional extra. He was not referring to the few droplets on the brow of an infant child, but the real, biblical form. What was good enough for the Ethiopian eunuch, the Philippian jailer, Saul of Tarsus and the Son of God was good enough for us.

'You,' concluded Pastor Anderson-Brown, sweeping his deepset brown eyes from ground floor to gallery, 'will want to follow the Lord through the waters of baptism!'

Nobody was likely to disagree with a pale young man with his soul on fire. Not on Sunday nights anyway. Monday mornings were apt to produce a different slant, but any Bethelite worthy of his salt had entered his name on the candidates' list on Sunday night. All that remained was to locate the waters of baptism, for the architect had not thought it necessary to design a baptistry when Lowesmoor Chapel was built.

'What is the matter with the Severn?' queried the minister, 'Baptism is supposed to be a public witness.'

The Severn it was. Our river compared quite favourably with the Jordan, though it was some years before I established this fact with my own eyes. The Severn was broad and clear by the time it reached our city from the Welsh mountains. It skirted the perimeter of the racecourse and flowed over the sloping deck of the 'barge' which was moored to the northern end. This was, in fact, no more than a submerged sloping platform surrounded on three sides by a canvas screen, but open to view from the river bank. The water depth varied from two and a half feet at the shallow end, to six feet. Wooden steps were provided both ends and a handrail ran just below the water surface.

The barge was heaven-sent for our purpose. What a mercy the riverside strollers of 1868 had not succeeded in their petition to the City Fathers asking for its removal! It was then the nearest thing the city had to a swimming bath and the early attempt to banish it arose only because few of its original clients could afford costumes or towels, and the Corporation could afford no dressing rooms. After a swim, the bathers had no alternative to a do-it-yourself spin-drying process up and down the river bank. This, in

the opinion of the riverside strollers, was no enhancement
to the view. Hence the petition.

Wisely the Corporation poured oil on troubled waters by
limiting the use of the bathing barge to specified hours
and posting a watchdog with orders, according to the city
archives, to bring for prosecution 'any person guilty of
unnecessary or indecent exposure.' This must have
provided a challenge to the watchdog's powers of
selectivity but, had he survived into the nineteen
twenties, he would have had no cause for worry on the
day when the Bethelites came down to the waters. We were
fully and suitably clothed. The barge cannot ever have
boasted more modest clients. I had a new white silk dress
for the occasion.

The idea of baptism being a public declaration of faith
had gained momentum when the pastor gave it his full
attention. He assembled us outside the church on the
appointed Saturday to form a Procession of Witness,
headed by two doughty souls bearing aloft a poster
proclaiming where we were from and what it was all about.
Next came the candidates in white, followed by the rank
and file. The choir girls in black and white uniforms
brought up the rear.

When all were satisfactorily lined up, Pastor
Anderson-Brown looked around for some church officer to
fall in with him in the lead, at which point my father
suddenly realized it was his duty to go on ahead and make
sure all preparations at the other end were as they should
be. Father was never one to parade his piety, and in any
case he had been baptised years before in the more
decorous setting of the Gospel Hall baptistry.

By the time we reached the top of Lowesmoor and filed
into the Foregate, the police were on hand to control
traffic. We reached the racecourse and crossed it to the
river bank, which was already filling with onlookers. The
concrete path surrounding the barge deck had been well
prepared. The length on the far side, nearest mid-stream,
held an improvised pulpit, a piano and choir seating, to all
of which their respective occupants filed. We who were
candidates took the length of platform at the foot of the
sloping grass bank, where we had been provided with
seats facing the water and across to the platform party on
the other side.

I glanced across at the pianist; Eva Collings was a
Grammar School girl, only a year or two older than myself.

Quiet and demure as she was, her playing was lively and versatile. She had to hear a tune only once and could pick it up on the keyboard in seconds, which was of tremendous value to a church where most of the community singing was spontaneous.

The singing and the preaching over, the pastor and his helper donned their baptismal gowns and special footwear. Choirmaster Anthony Allen who followed the pastor down the steps, was the brother of Jack Browning's wife, and I wondered if Jack was somewhere behind us on the bank, for he knew of our family's involvement and took a good natured interest therein. I did not suppose his mother would be there, Saturday being her best day for bike hire, but I was pretty sure I had glimpsed Olga's Uncle Bert at the top of the bank, astride his ice cream tricycle.

Now it was time for each candidate to move forward in turn, announce himself or herself, state the purpose and step into the water.

First to go was a bold young woman, whose courage had been shown several times as she stood with the 'open air' ring at street corners, which was then an acceptable and certainly inexpensive means of evangelism. Ada had a strong, unfaltering voice and was never at a loss for words. 'I am only a common factory girl,' she would declare, 'But I am here today to say what the Lord Jesus Christ has done for me.' Standing at the edge of the water she did not fail us and when she emerged, with streaming face and clothing, she looked exhilarated. It put heart into all of us. She had a gift for leadership.

As I awaited my turn, a cool breeze rustled the scalloped edge of my silk dress. It occurred to me then that when I first came to this place, in a swimming party of schoolgirls, I had unthinkingly stepped straight down into the water. It rose swiftly about my breast and left me helplessly gasping for breath, wondering if my lungs would ever function normally again. After that, even when I could swim, it had been the inch-by-inch method of entry into the water for me. I could see I should have to change my ideas today.

One by one the candidates went in, were met by helpers with towels and wrappings, and led up the bank to the changing rooms which our present day Corporation had thoughtfully provided. Then it was my turn. 'I'll take this one on my own,' the young pastor murmured as I arrived in the water. I gripped his left wrist as instructed and he slid his right arm around my shoulders –

On the confession of your faith, I baptise you in these waters in the name of the Father, and of the Son and of the Holy Ghost.

Swiftly he laid me back into the water for a second, then I was up and away. As I reached the changing rooms I realized with a start of surprise that I had not felt the slightest tremor of cold in the water. The press reported next day (we even got into one of the nationals), 'Among the baptismal candidates was a young blind woman who came out of the water with a smile on her shadowed features, and a schoolgirl of thirteen.' It was a 'public declaration' right enough!

* * * * *

It appeared I had taken the plunge in more ways than one. Taking me on one side a few days later, the pastor commented, 'You were quite good – in what you said as you were baptised. We'll have a Children's Service next month. You shall be the preacher!'

Four weeks later, as I took my place on a platform facing a crowded Sunday night audience, I realized what I had taken on. It was true I had contributed to a programme, with others, in a 'Crusader' weeknight meeting, but this was rather different. Boys and girls filled the platform to right and left of me. In the aisles chairs were added to accommodate latecomers. The minister seated himself at a vantage point from which he could cope with emergencies (wise man!) and we were away to a lusty start.

Singly or in groups the children took their cues and played their parts. The audience was encouraging and receptive, especially towards the tinies who looked unbelievably innocent. Contrarily those who were less well prepared, stumbled over their lines and stood in agonizing embarrassment, got a better reception than the word perfect! I was troubled for my young brother Ernest who had been bidden to recite 'The Trial of a Sinner', for I knew him to be a reluctant performer, but when the time came he fixed his eye on a spot in the gallery ceiling and went through without a hitch. Now I was left with nobody's predicament but my own to cope with...

During the last item before the address I tried to marshal my wandering thoughts. Surreptitiously I fingered the marked page in my Bible and glanced at my notes. I caught my breath to see how scanty they were! Last night, in prospect, the words had tumbled out, but now...? Concentration was failing and I sought inspiration from the remaining item. The choirmaster's little daughter was hoisted to a chair at the front of the platform, looking marvellous in a red dress and immaculate dark ringlets. Shirley Temple-like in appearance and performance, all sweetness and light, out came her words:

I washed my hands this morning, so very clean
and white;
I gave them up to Jesus to work with all my might.
Now little feet be careful just where you take me to,
Anywhere for Jesus, but only that will do!

I had heard them all too often in rehearsal and, as she wagged an admonishing finger towards her little white shoes, some curious mood of resentment and self doubt gripped me, so that I could not take even this last opportunity of recalling my own role.

Applause was not the done thing in church, but the responsive oh's and ah's inspired an encore. I welcomed the respite but not the words. I could never feel like that, I thought, so sweet and good! Not in a million years... What was I doing here? I didn't fit in. Would I ever? Did I want to? What on earth was I going to do?

Now Vic Collings, our boy M.C., was announcing me and I ascended the little winding staircase to the pulpit and shut the 'gate' behind me. The die was cast. I turned to face the audience, wearing my white silk dress, now with a black bow at the collar so that it matched up with the choir and 'Crusader' uniforms. In place of the black berets they favoured, I wore a white angora one, my hair hanging loosely around my shoulders. I probably looked younger than my years because I was small, round-faced and rather less sophisticated than some thirteen-year-olds. I think I knew it, but was glad because maybe less would be expected of me!

I had twenty minutes. Could I possibly last out? I read the Scripture portion slowly and clearly in case that was my limit... It was St John's account of the Feeding of the Five Thousand. Immediately the words took life. All thoughts of little Ivy's song and my own culpability faded as I re-read the key verse. I had chosen it as being appropriate to the service, rather than to me personally:

*There is a lad here which hath five barley loaves
and two small fishes; but what are they among
so many?*

I suppose the theme is obvious - this nameless lad, mentioned by only one of the Gospel writers, had wandered off into the Galilean Hills for a picnic and got mixed up with a miracle; we who were also nondescript and had little to offer might similarly, unexpectedly, prove to be a link in the chain leading to a divine demonstration.

As I tried to put across the thoughts I had prepared, I got a new exhilaration and my heart warmed up to the anonymous boy who, almost certainly, had not washed his hands for hours! Neither, when I came to think of it, had his 'little feet been careful just where they took him to.' He had slung together whatever he could get hold of to make a picnic pack, and had tagged on to a curious crowd, for no better reason than that he wanted to know what was going on. Contrary to the upbringing of all nice children, he had made himself both seen and heard - how else would they have known he had precisely five loaves and two small fishes?

I don't know how much I was able to put across to the listening audience - they were a warmhearted crowd - but unexpectedly I got a glow in my own soul that had not been there when I prepared this 'sermon'. The God who would pick up a hobble-de-hoy lad with an inquisitive mind through whom to fulfil His purpose - was just the one for me!

The audience was marvellous and the press kind. The feature concerning the 'Worcester Girl Preacher' got into one of the national papers (I think it was the Sketch). I felt a start of surprise to see my own naive round face looking up at me from newspaper print.

CHAPTER 11

Gospel Trail

MY FATHER'S youngest brother, Harry, carved out for himself a career that was somewhat novel and the envy of those who lived a humdrum existence. He became driver to a bookie. Grandmother, with considerable restraint, considering she had little time for Grandfather's involvement with the turf, purchased the car which conveyed the bookie to Epsom, Derby, Aintree and the rest. Thus Harry was often away for several days at a time, and home (with the car of course) for the days in between. Though he had not anticipated it, this became opportune as a means of transporting Bethelite supporters around the Midlands.

My debut as a girl preacher had brought in invitations to other Bethel churches in a radius of thirty miles or so - near enough for returning the same night if one was independent of public transport. Sometimes a dozen or so young folk would be available and willing to make up a programme, which was heartening for a preacher who was still uncertain of being able to completely fill the bill. The pastor could lay hands on a couple more cars on occasion and the party swung off in convoy, sometimes compiling the programme en route. It was not difficult to attract a good crowd in those days, even for a Gospel-orientated bill of fare. And such was the lively, generous appreciation of the audiences that it drew from one a corresponding freedom from restraint. I cannot be the first to discover that it is easier to speak to five hundred than to fifty... or to five, which is a challenge of a different nature altogether. And, of course, it is always easier away from 'home ground'.

To Harry our crowd must have provided a contrast to his other clientele, but he bore with us stoically on the Autumn evening when he chauffered us to Walsall, in the heart of the Black Country. As we neared our destination we glimpsed the belching smoke and ascending dust particles which clouded the skies above the tall foundry chimneys and gave this territory its foreign-sounding nickname. Thanks to periodic visits from Kit's West

Bromwich cousins (Grandfather's elder brother, Gus, had emigrated there from his native Malvern), our ears had become a little attuned to the different, rather beguiling accent of its industrious population.

Did they mind us calling their area, north of Birmingham, the Black Country, I wondered? They were a hearty, uninhibited people, proud of their muscular skills and the hundreds of large and small lucrative businesses which they built up with their crafts. We smiled instinctively at the honest, weatherbeaten grin of the entrepreneur who revelled in his recent successes. In anybody else it would have sounded boastful. 'I corrngoo wrong-g-g!' he declared. Somehow we wished him well and hoped it would always 'goo right' for him, though it seemed a lot to ask in this uncertain world.

Even the fair sex enjoyed prosperity as openly. We met a young mother who, having already inherited a tidy sum from a thrifty uncle, received news of more to follow, from another relative. 'I mayn to say,' she exclaimed, on sharing her news with us, 'Yo can allays do wi' a bit moah!'

But the crowd which awaited our arrival in the large central church in Walsall appeared to have set their sights a little higher, for they were singing a kind of 'warming up song' before the appointed time:

This is like heaven to me! This is like heaven to me!
I've passed over Jordan to Canaan's fair land –
And this is like heaven to me!

And how appropriate this was – for the strong influence of the Wesleys and their band of preachers from the West Country was still reflected in the baptismal registers. Those pages were sprinkled with Ezras, Calebs, Joshuas, Isaacs, Seths and Daniels. Named after Old Testament heroes, this revealed the hopeful expectations of godly parents. In many cases they were not disappointed. From these hardworking, often poorly educated families, had arisen many a local preacher who had left his mark. One went to town on the story of the Prodigal Son, we heard, graphically describing his advancing miseries along the downward slope – 'First he lost his overcoat.. then his jacket... then his shirt...' until he reached the climax of St Luke's story, the moment of repentance, 'When he came to *himself!*'

It was a wonder they wanted preachers from our more prosaic, reserved community, but they greeted us warmly enough through their small lively, energetic Welsh-born pastor, Matthew Francis. He greeted my father with great affection since here, he exclaimed, was somebody who would not look down upon him.

The church was already filled, the audience spilling over into spare chairs in the aisles, so Harry was obliged to find a seat with our party on the platform or stay outside in the cold. Knowing the likely length of our meetings, he elected for the platform. I glanced at him occasionally, hoping he was not feeling like a fish out of water. If my mother had her way, he would have landed in the Gospel net before this! Which was as much a mark of her affection as of her zeal.

One of Harry's engaging qualities was the rather embarrassed smile that played between his upper lip and sensitive nostrils, which was so natural to him that I was not a bit put out when he returned my querying glance with that upward quiver. He may have been reflecting that my preaching could hardly try him more than had my recent tentative exploratory efforts over Kit's keyboard to play 'The Song of the Volga Boatmen' with one finger. Harry was having a 'lie in' in the room above, following a late night journey home from Epsom. That 'Yo-o heave ho!' had a penetrating effect through ceiling rafters. Harry's protesting thumps on his bedroom floor came just as I had *almost* got the notes right, so I became as frustrated as he was.

But here on this Wednesday evening in the Black Country all went well. The Crusaders who provided the supporting programme ably fulfilled their role in settling the audience for the address, and we left home in higher spirits than when we set out. Our own pastor had made an 'appeal' for souls to yield to Jesus Christ 'as Saviour and Lord' and the response had been heartwarming.

* * * * *

We missed Harry, his large comfortable car and the back-up party, when invited to a weekend in Blackheath Bethel church. We had to make the best of public transport on the outward journey. Pastor Anderson-Brown undertook to procure a car and fetch my companion and me after church on the Sunday night and get us back home by midnight.

Leaving the railway station, we made our way towards the city centre, and I had the surprising experience of seeing my own face looking up at me from a muddy gutter. It was a discarded handbill with my photo advertising the weekend's meetings, adding in small print below my name 'accompanied by Miss George, also of Worcester.'

I glanced apologetically at Ada but she betrayed no reaction. This was the bold young woman who had stepped first into our baptismal pool. She had developed into a very good speaker. She had a crusading spirit and did not mind who knew it. Not being made of quite the same stuff, I felt a little diffident beside her, and quite rightly considered her to be the main speaker for this engagement. Perhaps I should not have worried. In her career as a lady gospeller, Ada had taken much more than this in her brisk stride, and she was a very heartening person to have at one's side.

Soon we encountered a party of young people handing out handbills and giving personal invitations to the meetings. We were asked to join them in an outdoor meeting, prior to the advertised ones. Ada excelled in these, having voice and demeanor which compelled attention. I did not contribute to the programme, though I suppose I fulfilled some function (unexpectedly) by being pointed out to listeners around the fringe as being the subject of their publicity. Maybe if I had then realized how brief is the finger of fame, I would not have felt so reluctant to acknowledge their warmhearted introductions.

At the end of the meetings in Blackheath, at which Ada and I spoke in turn, many of the audience were moved and responsive, and as I passed down the aisle towards the exit to shake hands with the departing crowd, one of the men intercepted me. He spoke animatedly about the meeting just ended and asked if he might pray with me. Courtesy impelled me to agree and he laid a hand upon each shoulder. As he concluded his impassioned prayer, a string of strange words came from his lips, a foreign tongue, quite unfamiliar to me, but which had a compelling force, a strange note of authority.

I did not realize it then, but it was my first encounter with the Pentecostals and the glossalia - but not the last. Oh, certainly not the last!

Unfortunately the car from Worcester met with some sort of hold up on the way to collect us from the pastor's

house at the end of that busy Sunday. We waited for some
hours, knowing that they could not begin the journey until
after the conclusion of the Lowesmoor services. Yet time
dragged on far beyond the expected hour. Most of the
household retired apologetically to bed and Pastor Perry
dozed off in his big armchair. Ada, who was old enough to
feel more responsible than I was, was on the verge of
tears. She was obliged to be at her factory bench by eight
o'clock on Monday morning and our own pastor had been
confident he could deliver us at our homes by midnight –
possibly unconsciously pressured by the name of Ada's
employers – the Cinderella Shoe manufacturers.

But Ada was concerned also on behalf of her elderly
parents. She was an 'only one' and they may not have
been in favour of her crusading activities with the
Bethelites. They were not fellow members, but their peace
of mind was important and it was likely they were not
reassured at their daughter's long delayed absence in the
hands of a very young minister/driver in a borrowed car.

Ada was seated on the opposite side of the hearth to
me, and I covertly studied her pretty red dress. Now she
was relieved of her confining beret and tweed-belted coat,
she looked feminine and more vulnerable. Her dark hair
curled around her temples above her now more softened
eyes as she dabbed an escaping tear. So... Crusaders
have tender hearts too?

At one a.m. Pastor Perry came to, jumped to his feet
and went to answer the loud knock on his door. We held
our breath. Was it a policeman? I made for the door too,
and heard voices.

'Thank God, brother,' exclaimed Pastor Perry heartily
as he greeted his fellow cleric, 'We were about to have a
baptism of tears!'

CHAPTER 12

An Alabaster Box

THE CAMARADERIE and more varied scope of the new Commercial School were much better suited to my temperament and resources than would have been the Girls' Grammar. (Their Head was very much a lady and would not have approved of my out-of-school activities). Staff and scholars alike were feeling their way into a new environment. Students came from all over the city and were more diverse in age and sophistication than those I had been accustomed to. Some of the girls in my own form were almost unrecognizable on Saturday mornings in high heels, furs and lipstick, for we were a fairly wide age group in that opening year.

For most, if not all, co-education was a new experience, and being housed under the same roof as the Technical School, girls were outnumbered by boys in a ratio of three to one - a very satisfactory arrangement. The younger male teachers had not taught girls before and gave us the cottonwool treatment, venting any accumulated wrath or exasperation upon their own sex. This was very gratifying while it lasted, and helped to offset the disconcerting effect of being provided with a Health and Beauty enthusiast half way through our second term.

Having managed perfectly well for more than six months with the necessary exercise provided by our brisk progress on foot or bike from all quarters of the city, not to mention the traffic along innumerable corridors once inside the Victoria Institute, we saw little need for the advent of Mrs Connell. Neither had we been warned in the list of 'requirements' provided by the headmaster of our joint Commercial and Technical Schools, to provide ourselves with gym dresses. However, eventually, in Assembly Hall, tubular chairs stacked away and doors bolted against Peeping Toms, we were at the newcomer's mercy, divested of our navy blue pleated tunics and white blouses. Very vulnerable!

Mrs C. was tall, lithe and brisk. Clad in a pale green Grecian-style short dress she moved like a panther, as if balanced on a perpetual springboard. Aloft on the dais at the far end of the hall which was normally graced by a dignified cap-and-gowned headmaster, she stood rocking from heel to toe and surveyed us imperiously. Being small I had the misfortune to be appointed to the front row and got a taste of 'that fierce light which beats upon a throne.'

It would have been better if someone had confided to me in earlier years that when standing at ease you have to distribute your weight equally on both feet. This would have saved my first pitfall. Unknowingly I repeated the error and Mrs C. took it as a personal slight without explaining her point of view. It is my conviction that when you have before you persons who persists in error, you might assume they do not know what they ought to know, and you should toss off the required information in words of not more than two syllables, as if merely in the way of a reminder. This gives the offenders time to cotton on, come to, correct themselves and give you henceforth not only their slavish co-operation but also their goodwill!

Mrs Connell, presumably, had not taken a degree in psychology while earning her P.T. qualification. No subsequent effort on my part could ever wipe my early defect from her memory. It is not a good thing to get off on the wrong foot with anybody, be it right or left, but presumably it is an experience which must be endured from time to time.

Happily the young University graduate appointed as our form master treated all girls with respect and inclined one to the view that the spirit of King Arthur and the Knights of the Round Table was not yet dead. Mr Cant was tall, dark and dignified, as well as being a rugger player of no mean repute. From him I could soak up information like a sponge.

Under Mr Cant I found a new pleasure in stringing words together. Odd phrases would jingle through my head unbidden, like melodies in the memory of the musically minded. Prose and verse were no longer the source of repetetive jargon. Gone forever was the dispiriting drone of thirty or forty voices chanting in unison to a bored teacher, bringing splendid lines into contempt through over-familiarity. The advent of the drama group opened up new vistas, though I looked anxiously over my shoulder lest I should be led into worldly paths. I was saved from that temptation, in all probability, because it became my inescapable fate to be saddled with child parts! 'God moves in a mysterious way...'

It is true that the school atmosphere appeared a little more 'pagan' than I had earlier experienced. We had no morning prayers or religious instruction. Yet the odd phrases and extracts from the Scriptures which cropped up in English Literature were like jewels set against a plain backcloth, and the more beautiful because of it.

The letters after Mr Cant's surname indicated that he held a degree in Eng. Litt. but the ones which preceded it were more of a mystery to us. His initials were Q.C. and by these he was known, behind his back. Mabel Morris declared they stood for Quinton Caractus but nobody knew where she got her information from. She could be right, I thought, for the names were distinctive and nicely suited to his air of nobility. But then, nothing about him could be wrong for me...

He was unlike any teacher I had known before, athletic, clever courteous and scholarly. Perhaps more of a scholar than a teacher? But to those who wanted to learn he could get information across. To the unwilling, at times, he may have been slightly inarticulate - but even that had compensations. On the morning when he was interpreting a French phrase on the blackboard which ran the length of the wall behind him, he paused for a word, half turned and tried over one or two likely ones. Involuntarily a more appropriate one escaped my lips, unrequested, from the front row. I clapped my hand to my mouth. Mr Cant smiled faintly and without even glancing in my direction, swiftly wrote the word on the board. When my blush had subsided I felt better than when my name had gone on the Honours Board eighteen months earlier!

First year French opened up new vistas in that delightful language which can turn a mundane word like 'window' into the gentle sound, as if borne on a soft wind, of 'fenêtre', which inclines you to take a hopeful view of our neighbour-country. It is disillusioning, of course, to discover on your first trip to improve your pronunciation, that the French do not seem to see much to admire in the English (The Commandant of our camp was less than gracious). But this is probably the fault of Henry Plantagenet who, before succeeding to the English throne, paid court to the powerful heiress, Eleanor of Acquitaine, when she was already married to the French king. Furthermore he kept the unfortunate Louis in total ignorance of his aspirations until after their banns were called (within a few days of her divorce) and thus annexed almost the whole of Western France for what was really the first British Empire, back in the twelfth century.

Henry brought Eleanor to our Cathedral for their coronation. This seems rather gracious of him since we fought for Stephen, his rival for the English throne, a few years earlier. Or was he rubbing it in? Either way the Worcester coronation must have been an impressive occasion, for history records that after returning from our High Altar they 'put away their crowns, vowing never to wear them again.'

I puzzled over this for a while until singing in this Cathedral at a later date the famous 'Love Divine, all loves excelling' which concludes -

Changed from glory into glory,
Till in heaven we take our place,
Till we cast our crowns before Thee,
Lost in wonder, love and praise.

The royal couple did not of course have the benefit of
Wesley's hymn, nor the sight of the magnificent altar
screen depicting Christ in Majesty, but were possibly
stirred by the same emotions. If so, what a pity they did
not return to this sanctuary more often to savour again
those tender moments. It would have saved them both
much unhappiness in the years ahead. There's a lot to be
said for regular church-going as a means of keeping oil in
your lamp, despite the claims of the 'We-can-worship-God-in-
the-great-outdoors' brigade.

There is nothing new under the sun! Their happiness
was wrecked by troublesome boys (King John was one of
them), which brings me to the afternoon which is printed
indelibly on my memory. There probably remained only half
an hour to the close of the school day, and Mr Cant was
trying to put across a difficult lesson. His concentration
was impaired, as he sought to illustrate some point on the
blackboard. He wheeled round more than once without
detecting the source of whispers and giggles in (I think)
the back row. A second later a folded scrap of paper
whizzed past my right eye and struck the tip of my nose
before dropping to my desk with a slight plop, for it was
weighted across the fold with a paper clip. I smothered a
slight gasp and covered it as Mr Cant swung round for
the last time.

'I've had enough,' he announced grimly, and caught my
near neighbour grinning. 'You,' he told the boy, 'can take
a detention on Friday. Report to me then after school.' He
slammed his books into his desk, drew his gown more
closely around his shoulders and strode to the door.

The momentary awkward silence was soon broken,
though the class thought it politic to remain behind the
closed door until their usual emerging time. I smoothed out
the offending scrap of paper and found a scrawled message
- 'Come to the flicks with me next Friday after school?' It
was signed 'H' who happened to be the offender whose
name Mr Cant had rapidly entered in his little black
punishment book before departing. So it needed no reply.
As we left the form room I glanced briefly at him. He
shrugged nonchalantly.

But the little black book was never handed in to the master who was to preside over the detention class that Friday. On his way home from playing rugger astride his motorcycle, our form master ran into another vehicle. His injuries were serious and surgeons fought to save a leg. Two days later we heard the limb had to be amputated, followed by a further report that gangrene had set in. Then came news that the limb had been sacrificed in vain. We would see Mr Cant no more. Our last link with him was his family's acknowledgment of the funeral flowers to which we had subscribed. My only personal 'legacy' was the summing up in his firm handwriting at the foot of my last end-of-term report: 'a promising start. Q.C.C.' I kept it for a long time...

On the Friday ending that school week, the writer of the note which had been flicked across to me stopped me in the corridor. 'What about it then?' he asked, 'You know - the flicks!'

'But you've got a detention,' I pointed out.

'Not now,' he said, 'I've been to look at the list and my name's not on it. I reckon Q.C. never gave it in. Nobody will know!'

I looked at him with loathing. 'I wouldn't dream of coming,' I said, 'And you... you're an unfeeling pig! You should go.'

'You must be nuts,' he ejaculated. 'Doing detention won't do anything for Cant! What's the idea? Have you got a pash on him? Would you go?'

'Yes, I would,' I answered shortly and left him before he could ask me why. If I had been obliged to express my feelings by some visible token, I think it would not have been by a red rose. Something more akin to... an alabaster box perhaps?

Without even noticing it, I had passed up my first 'date' without the slightest regret.

* * * * *

Our second and last year at the school was not without event either. Despite the fact that my parents' sixth and last child was on the way, I had never concerned myself with the mysteries behind these events. There were many more interesting matters to occupy one's mind. But one of the girls, being daughter to a midwife and in consultation with others, thought it necessary to remedy this defect in

my education. We were walking home down Pierpoint
Street, a thoroughfare of tall old buildings given over
mainly to solicitors' offices and an unlikely place in which
to receive a revelation. I was not sure that I had rightly
understood Marjorie and took refuge in silence, deciding
this was the moment to cross the road and engage myself
with passing traffic. Uncertainly Marjorie tried to pursue
the topic, but I made some perfunctory excuse and ran
home. It was not a matter on which I was disposed to ask
questions, even of my mother, and when I broached the
difficult subject to Kit I found she did not relish the topic
but had come to terms with it over the years. I felt better
once the sickness had passed off.

According to today's sex educators my ignorance put me
in jeopardy. Yet I think if the subject had been broached
to me in less desirable circumstances, my reaction would
have been an instinctive rejection. In innocence there is a
kind of defence - a natural modesty.

Fortunately our new baby was so pretty and so winsome
that she offset for me some of the sense of shock. The
pretty nurse from our church who spent off-duty hours
with us appealed to my mother to name this last child
Jean. Mother amplified this by calling her 'the flower of
the flock' which, apart from being no compliment to the
rest of us, seemed a curious association of vegetable and
animal. Her arrival in December added a pleasing,
sentimental touch to the season's preparations. Girls from
the church came to drool over the new baby and help
dress our tree.

Nostalgia was very much in the air that month. At our
end-of-term Christmas Concert given in the school Lecture
Theatre one of the senior boys cleverly parodied a
well-known song so that the verses featured recognizable
personalities present, mainly teachers. The auditorium was
designed amphitheatre-style so that however small you
were you got a reasonable view. I mentally blessed the
designer (the Romans thought of it long ago) and in a
spirit of euphoria I looked down upon the black-gowned
staff on the platform, trying not to dwell too much upon
the one who was missing this year. I gave my attention to
the minstrel party fronting the stage, and did not at first
recognize that I was the subject of their last verse! I had
never borne up well under teasing but the warm Yuletide
atmosphere and the good-natured, back-slapping banter as
we all swung into the chorus '...singing Polly-wolly-doodle

all the day' combined to disarm me and to give me a brief taste of how very pleasant it is to be accepted by one's peers...

Yet I was not at all sure I liked my new nickname until the Spring number of the school magazine, edited by one Reg Cooke, came off the press. I was mollified. The editorial ran:

> We cannot confirm the statement that someone is attempting to split the atom. This however does not refer to the 'Mighty Atom' and we are in no danger of losing a school favourite. We do not know whether the aforementioned has any stored up energy, but she is easily holding her own against comparatively gigantic tormentors!

CHAPTER 13

Pitmans Progress

*His letters, say they, are weighty and powerful;
but his bodily presence is weak and his speech
contemptible.*

I LAUGHED spontaneously when I read the words, written
by Paul to the converts at Corinth, though I did think, on
reflection, that it was no credit to the Corinthians that
they had let him know when his personal appearance did
not come up to the expectations aroused by his letter
writing. With friends like that, who needs the Pharisees
and the Sadducees? It was when I found myself nibbling at
the same humble pie that St Paul got my full sympathy in
this regard.

In our final school term we were coached in the art of
writing legible but cringing letters designed to move the
hearts of Worcester industrialists into the belief that we
were assets they should acquire. Despite our R.S.A.
certificates in commerce, it was not easy to land a job in
1932, even if one was willing to give forty two and a half
hours of earnest endeavour for eight, ten or (at most)
twelve shillings a week, take-it-or-leave-it. Most people
took it, even the seventeen and eighteen year olds. I was
not yet sixteen.

Most of my applications yielded me the privilege of the
personal interview for which I had dutifully 'begged', and
time off from school was automatically allowed. Then came
the crunch! Sitting in a waiting room with other hopeful
candidates, I looked covertly around at the pert little
misses with fashionable, bobbed hair, lipstick and high
heels. Was it likely the boss would select a round-faced
freckled child with a bunch of sandy hair tied at the back
- even with proffered speeds of 120 and 60 words per
minute?

'Not all employers are beguiled by a pretty face,'
somebody had tried (without tact) to reassure me. But I
had time to reflect while waiting there that though this
employer might be impervious to personal charms, he might
think it better for his business prestige to have a more

sophisticated girl in his receptionist's office, looking for all the world as though he paid her twice as much as the 'ten bob' she probably drew. Confidence was apt to evaporate before his unsmiling secretary opened the door and said, 'Miss Lawrence - will you go in please?'

'You are... er... rather petite,' suggested one elderly interviewer, doubtfully surveying my awkward perch on the abnormally high stool provided for the typing test. Truly it was rather Dickensian in that office with its brown paintwork, tatty linoleum and a typewriter placed on a table surface much higher than a purpose-built typist's desk. I slid off while he spiralled the stool anti-clockwise until I could touch the floor with my toes. He left me typing with elbows well below table-top level which, as any girl will tell you, is not calculated to win you trophies as the Secretary of the Year. I failed to get that job, but in retrospect came to appreciate the interviewer's courtesy.

'Aye, aye!' exclaimed one hearty type, a self-made man with a 'Brummie' accent. 'Yo want t' git some muck in y' shoes!' I was offended and mystified. Though I grew up in an agricultural county, it was years before I glimpsed the obvious connection between muck and fertilizer.

After two or three unsuccessful interviews I scoured Worcester for a pair of high-heeled shoes in (ladies) size 2 - and found I had begun a search which would dog my footsteps for the rest of my life. Despite our city boasting of the Cinderella Shoe Factory, I failed to track down at any of the local shops anything which would add two or three inches to my height. Most styles have a range of three to seven. It was just possible, I found, by the use of heel-grips, shoe liners and will power to stay put in a pair of shoes one size larger than my feet. But there is a distinct risk, if ever you have to run for a 'bus, that you will stumble up the steps in stockinged feet!

'Oh, dear,' my mother sighed, 'Perhaps I over-did it,' confessing that she had a weakness for dainty feet and had ignored the advice and example of her sisters - to buy children's shoes in a size that would allow for growth. 'It seemed to me,' she explained in her own defence, 'when their shoes shone, they were "sloppy"; when eventually they fitted, they were shabby!' It had a certain logic and I ceased to equate her with the Chinese mothers, who bound their daughters' feet to keep them tiny!

Never one to suffer in silence, I complained to local shops. 'I've seen a catalogue where the size range is from

2 - 8.'

'Maybe,' replied one manager, 'but we only stock the sizes we can sell locally - move to Wales, dearie, our Welsh branches stock your size.'

It was a comfort to find I was not a freak, but I was astonished at this indication that the Welsh had small feet - despite all that rarebit, mutton, cheese and creamy butter. And they so content and homely in voluminous skirts, big white aprons and tall black hats! *They* traversed the hills and the valleys on dainty feet?

So I used my catalogue and sent to a mail order firm. It was worth the trouble - those heels added dignity as well as inches! I felt a glow of goodwill toward footwear manufacturers, and thought bemusedly of Lady Jane Grey, our 'nine days queen'. Even in Tudor times they made her little court shoes with built-up heels. If one had to tread the path to the scaffold when only sixteen years old, how much better to do so 'walking tall'. This may have contributed to her superb presence of mind when approaching the block. Tucking in her collar and neckline, she bequeathed her dress to her maid, 'for it is of good stuff,' she pointed out. I wonder what became of her little shoes?

Compared with this, my ordeal, when the appointment came, was negligible. Three-thirty was the stipulated time, and at three o'clock I left school, slipping on my new shoes in readiness, only to find on arrival that Irene Taylor was there before me - she having had the foresight to skip afternoon school, going home to change into her weekend clothes. Of all the girls in our school year, though she was a member of the 'B' stream, Irene was the one most calculated to give a person an inferiority complex. From her smart little felt toque with the peacock feather affixed to the upturned brim, her carelessly slung fox fur around one shoulder, her trim tweed 'two-piece', down to her silk stockings and crocodile skin shoes, she was a 5'6" 'flapper'. That she was good-looking, even before the skilfully applied make-up, goes without saying.

She was seated alongside a girl in a dark dress and Grammar School blazer, and gave me a cursory nod. As we waited my heart sank down into my new shoes. When we had first arrived at the Commercial School almost two years earlier, this girl had drawn a coterie around her instantly. Whereas most of us made the best of Marks & Spencer poplin, she sported a silk blouse with more shapely collar.

Our serge gym tunics with pleats that soon commenced to slacken near the hemline could not compete with navy alpaca having permanent knife pleats... Even if I had run home on that day of the interview to change, the fur fabric coat made out of Mother's opera cloak would not have intimidated Irene. The clock ticked on. She went in before me and betrayed neither triumph nor disaster when she emerged from the inner sanctum twenty minutes later.

But - wonder of wonders - I landed the job, with a large engineering firm on the fringe of Lowesmoor, and tasted the elixir of having a little money in the pocket. On the first Saturday afternoon after pay day (we worked in the mornings of course) I walked up and down every aisle in Woolworths, true then to their slogan 'Nothing over Sixpence.' You could not find a better place to assess your spending power!

Alas... there is a price to every victory. My first six months 'in business' was a difficult time, way beyond the normal transition from schoolroom to office desk. I coped fairly well with the changeover from a varied school curriculum to one long maths lesson as I learned to extract from the works time sheets the number of hours spent on each contract, and to translate those into financial costing - though figures had not hitherto been my forte. But the country was still in recession and one was thankful for a job.

Yet, as the other three 'female clerks' were several years older than I was, and were related to personalities on the firm's management, I was conscious of being the 'odd one out'. I became aware that the office second-in-command was more familiar with my family background and past activities than was convenient. He and the chief clerk enlivened the office by remarks of a personal nature and with questions addressed to me which baffled me. Those I could not grasp made me ill at ease, and I felt even worse when a glimmer of meaning penetrated my unwilling consciousness. Had I been the staff member shortly to become a bride I doubt if I could have gone on with the marriage!

I suppose I was a prude by their standards, maybe rather precocious and now developing a growing sensitiveness. 'Must have been a good collection at Lowesmoor Chapel last night' was the only comment my new pretty tweed coat aroused, followed by loudly whispered speculations as to whether my father was treasurer as well as secretary there. On it went, week after week, but chiefly it was the double meanings which troubled me. I found myself being trapped into answering apparently innocent questions.

'It really is too bad,' sympathized Kit with the wry grimace which was characteristic of her ability to convey feeling. Recognizing that my troubles were on a different level to those encountered by herself with the formidable Miss Baskerville, she felt ill-equipped to offer advice. 'Perhaps you should complain to the chief clerk,' she suggested, but with reluctance, for whatever else Harry Wharton, Tom Merry & Co. had taught us, we had grasped that sneaking was the unforgiveable sin. 'But after all,' she added in justification, 'the chief clerk should set the tone of the place.' 'But he does,' I sighed, 'That's the trouble!'

Quite suddenly the situation came to a head, and from an unexpected quarter. Robert, a young fellow who had hitherto earned my ungrudging respect because he did not appear to participate in the unsavoury 'jokes' proved to be the last straw.

Well, actually it was Robert and the mouse.

The poor little creature had run his earthly course before I saw him and deserved better than to be put on display over Robert's desk (immediately in front of mine) and coloured with red ink.

I exerted all my willpower to concentrate upon the columns of figures before me, but it was a losing battle. Fifteen minutes before lunchtime break I shuffled my papers into place, opened my desk and took out my handbag and gloves. 'I'm going downstairs,' I informed the chief clerk, reckless now of all consequences, 'and I will not come back up here until I know that... that... has been removed.'

It goes without saying perhaps that I could not eat a thing, even downstairs with Christine, the Accountant's secretary. 'It can't hurt you, duckie,' she pointed out reasonably enough, but I stuck to my guns. 'I'm not going back up there until I know it's gone.' When work was resumed for the afternoon she trailed off upstairs, returning a few moments later. 'Alright,' she said, indicating the stairs, 'It's gone.'

I knew I could trust her so I went, but avoided looking at the others or at the wall. I sat down, slid open my desk drawer to put in my bag and gloves - and there it was!

I could stand no more, gathered up my bag and fled down to Christine. 'I want to see the Accountant' I said, 'I won't go back up there until I have.' 'You'll have to wait until the Kalamazoo rep. goes,' warned Christine.

I had no idea what I would say. Apart from the odious sin of 'sneaking', so disdained by The Gem and The Magnet, I could not have borne to recount what I had been through. Dare I give in my notice? It was considered the height of irresponsibility to change jobs within five years in those days - even if one could. Finally the door opened. 'Go in,' said Christine, 'and - good luck!'

The Accountant, the very same who had appointed me six months earlier, waived me to a chair courteously, propped his elbows on the desk and pressed together the tips of his fingers. As I opened my mouth, he took the initiative.

'Ah now, I am glad to see you,' he began, 'I have a proposition to put to you. A young lady in the typing department, a niece of one of our departmental managers, has found that shorthand and typing is not her forte. In fact, she has been absent for a few weeks with a nervous breakdown. She wants to return to the firm, but with a different job. Would you consider an exchange with her? It would be a possible solution.'

It was the perfect solution. I took to the typing pool like a duck to water. Shorthand with its curves, dots and dashes has always had a fascination for me even as an art form. I had learned to type by touch (blindfolded) and rhythmically (to music), and it goes without saying that these are assets of no mean merit to a person who likes putting thoughts on paper.

A typing pool is not Utopia, of course. It is not easy to divide work equally between twenty or more females of differing ages, capabilities and temperaments, so there are undercurrents. Furthermore, the temperature rises sharply between four and five o'clock, at which time the departmental bosses discover they have urgent matters to communicate by that evening's post. All now becomes a hotbed of endeavour. Everybody - or nearly everybody - is galvanised into activity. The odd one or two who are idle earn the growing disfavour of the rest, particularly if they do not come up with offers of envelope-typing, page checking and other menial aids to those pressed beyond measure. It is one thing to be pounding typewriter keys against the clock, but to do so when glimpsing from the corner of one's furious eye that one's neighbour is manicuring her nails, calls for a sweetness of disposition that is lacking in most of us.

Not surprisingly things go wrong under pressure. Feelings run high. Exasperation finds expression in unladylike words. The air is tinged with blue, but those girls had hearts of gold. I was allowed a first 'read' of her 'Woman's Weekly' by one whose pages I sorted and stapled. I willingly collected it for her each Tuesday lunchtime as I cycled back through Lowesmoor, and bought myself a Mars bar at the same time. The two combined deliciously in the odd ten or twenty minutes that might be spared in the early afternoon, and the choice of both has been endorsed over more than fifty years of reading and chewing by a discriminating public.

Spending seven or more hours a day in the company of the same dozen girls calls for a certain amount of involvement, and it was fascinating to watch the development of their romances, the introspection caused by hesitation - whether to make the best of the bird-in-hand... etc... and the coming to terms when, either way, there was no choice. It was not then considered the done thing for a fellow to terminate a romance - he was nothing short of a cad if he did - but a girl had to educate herself in reading the signs and deciding when to let go. A little temporary vacillating might be allowed without loss of face, but there had to be a limit. Debate hinged upon whether time was ripe to hold the ship steady, steer it into calmer waters, or to take to the lifeboat in the hope of making for another desired haven before it was too late. It was as good as anything in the Woman's Weekly!

So there was a camaraderie among the group of girls which was an education in itself. Though my life differed from theirs in some respects, their teasing was good natured and it was good to share with them progress and problems on the typing front, especially on the occasions when a group would unite in an endeavour to translate some girl's shorthand outline which she utterly failed to discern or recall. We would try everything to prompt her memory in the hope of sparing her the ordeal of confessing to some irascible engineer that she had come to a halt in an involved letter or tender. We regarded every pencilled stroke and dot, however outlandishly scrawled, as though it were the clue to a treasure hunt in the South Pacific. It was better than a crossword puzzle and certainly more rewarding if you had the wit to come up with the elusive 'bon mot'.

CHAPTER 14

Roving Commission

INEVITABLY I acquired a new nickname. The milestones in my life could well have been inscribed by a series of them. 'Sister Aimee' was this latest one. It was not at first unwelcome. Only by contrasting her life with mine did I realize the incongruity of it.

Aimee Semple MacPherson was a well-known evangelist in the U.S.A. To be recognized as an evangelist a person has to be pretty good on a platform – and a woman twice as good. Married first to Robert Semple, a missionary who died soon after their arrival in India, the young widow returned to the States and became noted for her undoubted ability to hold an audience. Forthright and dramatic in expression, she worked mainly in Los Angeles. She attracted many of the film celebrities to her own Angelus Temple, and they must have recognized in her many of the qualities it takes to hold a crowd. Hers must have been a more outstanding personality than many of theirs for she was actress, scriptwriter, producer, director all in one.

Aimee founded her own group of Foursquare Churches, of which Angelus Temple, seating several thousand, was the H.Q., employing two or three assistant pastors, an orchestra and a choir attractively robed. In some degree she was years ahead of her time. Her lighting effects and other aids were considered ostentatious by most religious organizations then. On the platform she wore a satin cloak of (I think) royal blue lined with scarlet, fastened at her left shoulder with a beautiful clasp. Her wealth of auburn hair was piled on top of her head and she was not averse to a little, well applied make-up.

Much of this would have been embarrassing to her British hosts when she appeared at the Royal Albert Hall around 1926. In evangelical circles in Britain make-up was associated with the 'painted Jezebel' who intimidated the prophet Elijah and who came (dare I say it?) to such a sticky end – while hats were a 'must' for God-fearing ladies in line with a very straight injunction from St Paul who saw therein a token of demurity.

So Mrs MacPherson (the surname was her second husband's) was a law unto herself, gifted, outstanding, successful and sincere according to reliable evidence, yet with a flamboyance unpopular with the British. Yet, such was the goodwill of the girls in the typing pool, that I am sure the nickname was not intended to be ironic. Over the next several years they treated me with something rather warmer than tolerance.

One dark, vivid girl was especially friendly towards me. Bigger and some years older than I was, I did not feel offended when she dropped into the rather familiar epithet of 'Little un.' Her language under stress left a lot to be desired, but she it was who helped me beat the clock one Saturday morning. I was booked for a weekend of meetings and my train left at 1.15 from Shrub Hill Station about five hundred yards away. It was fixed for me to go straight to the station from the office where we finished work at one o'clock. My suitcase, ready packed at home, was to be brought to me there by my schoolboy brother. I was poised for flight.

Then at 12.30 I was summoned aloft by a man whose life apparently depended upon a letter being typed that very morning. In secret despair I scribbled down the outlines and fled below at the double. Alas – nothing would go right! My neighbouring, dark-haired angel, after five fruitless minutes spent in trying to help me pound the words on to paper, flew upstairs to confront the astonished engineer with the news that if he did not forego his letter that morning a congregation would be without a preacher that evening! Never having encountered this situation before, the man had no defence and capitulated just as the suitcase arrived on Ernest's bike.

Marvellous! Though it would never have done for the real Sister Aimee!

It was a pity our Worcester pastor did not know that Bristol's Temple Meads Station had about a dozen exits. Arrangements for my weekend engagement at the Bethel Temple there had all been made hurriedly by telegram, for few people of our acquaintance had telephones. Doubtless the economy in words had resulted in my dilemma. No precise plan had been made for a meeting place. I wandered along the platform, trailing my weekend case, and encountered nobody who looked like a church secretary. As I was now sixteen I presume it had been thought I had enough intelligence to travel alone. Reluctant to disillusion anybody on this point, I wandered off the station and picked my way towards the city centre.

Bristol was a bigger place than I imagined. I had no address to make for as my host was to meet me, but I knew a Bible College had been opened by the Bethel Evangelistic Society somewhere in the vicinity. A year earlier, when I was still at school, Pastor Edward Jeffreys had visited our home and had a conference with the local pastor and my father on some administration matters. It also ensued that he showed some interest in my activities (reports appeared in the Society's magazine) and suggested a possible opening for me in the office at Bristol when I had a little experience, combining secretarial work with College studies. This might show whether my future might lie in either direction.

I was excited at the prospect. I fear I had a weakness for compromise and to join the college in a dual capacity seemed to insure one against failure... There was also the trifling advantage in such a setting of meeting personable young men cloistered away from the rival charms of other girls. I maintained that at this stage of my life marriage was not the be all and the end all – in fact my party pieces at Grandmother's annual family gatherings were firmly of the 'Oh, no John, no-o John, no-o John, no!' variety. But one cannot be blamed for wanting the chance to say No. This visit to Bristol, unexpectedly offered when some previous programme fell through, might well pave the way!

Unfortunately the college was in recess for the long summer break, so I made for Milk Street where I knew the mother church of the movement to be, tracking it down by frequent enquiry. The notice board confirmed that a girl preacher from Worcester would occupy the pulpit, but I could trace no address or phone number to contact. None of the civic offices would be open where I could make enquiries about responsible personnel, and I had no recourse but to make for the nearest police station.

At the sergeant's desk I waited while he tried to answer two telephones at once. Eventually, adopting a patient expression he peered at me over the high counter. 'I'm afraid I'm lost,' I confessed, 'I've come from Worcester and was expecting to be met at the station.'

'Who was supposed to meet you?' was his query.

'I'm not aware of the person's name, sergeant, but he is secretary to the Bethel Church in Milk Street. I must find him as soon as possible. I - I've come to take the weekend services.'

'Oh, I see,' he answered slowly, in the manner of one who plainly did not, but in the absence of any better

explanation he apparently gave me the benefit of the doubt. He sent his minions scurrying hither and thither in an effort to dispose of me. Meanwhile I was escorted to a little room at the rear and fed on tea and biscuits. The bobbies eyed me quizzically.

Two or three hours passed with no greater diversion than an occasional visit from the boys in blue to see if I was still there. The sergeant was in favour of sending me to a Y.W.C.A. hostel for the night, but I clung stubbornly to the hope they would find my host. I had the feeling the trail would go cold if I was removed from their sight.

I think I was right, but it was after eleven at night when they traced a weary man in his mid-thirties, exhausted from fruitless enquiries at the railway station and preparing for bed. I had fallen asleep in that back room by the time the secretary and his wife came to collect

me. I came to with a start at the sound of a foreign accent
talking excitedly, and was gathered up by a charming
Frenchwoman wearing a fur coat over a pretty shell-pink
nightdress. I was almost home and dry, and could afford
now to smile at the station sergeant's confession to my
driver that he had not taken me seriously for some time. I
looked rather less than my sixteen years, and my naivety
at landing in such a predicament scarcely gave credence to
my appointment as a visiting preacher!

Next morning all was well at Milk Street. If I was to
blame for the fracas of the previous day (and quite a
search party had been summoned) nobody entertained any
rancour. The people were, as so often I found, most kind
and receptive. I fulfilled what was required of me, and
was generously invited to stay on for a brief visit to the
coast at Dawlish with my host, his attractive French wife
and their daughter Juliet.

In Stoke on Trent a few weeks later I stayed with the
local minister and was met without difficulty. On arriving
at the manse I mentally pulled up my socks and hoped I
could conduct myself becomingly under this auspicious roof
- a far greater hazard than preaching from a pulpit!

The pastor was out on some business. His wife was
preparing the mid-day meal. She nodded to me a little
perfunctorily I thought, and after freshening up I
ventured down to the dining room. From the adjoining
kitchen I could hear voices, both Welsh accented, and both
raised.

'I tell you, Megan' came the voice of the minister's
wife, 'I won't have it - so there! Pan Yan I said and Pan
Yan I meant!'

There followed some sort of protest, half hysterical but
indistinguishable. The pastor's wife broke in again -

'No look you here, Megan - there's no two ways about
it! Your father will take no other pickle than Pan Yan and
no old grocer is going to palm off his rubbish on me!
Straight back to that Davis you go and take that jar back.
If you don't do it quick now, it's a clout you'll be getting
to show you how!'

I felt a bit hot under the collar and wondered if I
should get back upstairs before it was known that I had
overheard, but Mrs Parry bustled into the dining room
seconds later and was not a whit abashed to find me
there. She continued her remonstrance through the half
open door of the kitchen, as a big, fair haired girl

entered disconsolately. She was still tearful and barely paused for an introduction.

'Cold meat it is today, it being Saturday,' announced Mrs Parry as she placed the cutlery around her table, 'and Megan's dad must have his pickles with cold beef.' But Megan here has to go and bring the wrong brand. It's Pan Yan we always have, and Pan Yan we always shall. She shall take that back to Davis, the corner shop and get it changed. Now off with you Megan before your father comes in and we sit to the meal.'

I interrupted the fresh flow of tears with an offer to do the errand or accompany Megan to lend my weight. Mrs Parry was not particular who went, but her sense of discipline was better satisfied by insisting that Megan came to identify the erring Davis. Megan and I returned in triumph and the cold meat met its fate suitably spiced. Pastor Parry was a large, rubicund man with the easy, genial manner of Welsh pastors, which went some way toward dispelling the rather 'flat' feeling which had overtaken my evangelical zeal.

The church was large, well organized and had a good choir trained by an ex-Salvation Army officer. The girls, as in Worcester, wore white dresses, piped with black braid, and black berets. My own white dress and beret came into its own again.

We arrived early and found many of the audience already waiting. Their warmth did something to offset Mrs Parry's cool reception and the deflating effect of the contretemps over the pastor's pickles. Many, particularly youngsters, came forward with autograph books or Bible fly-leaves for signature. In Worcester we were not too keen on this kind of thing, but I felt it would have been churlish to refuse and maybe would have aroused a feeling of restraint when I so badly needed goodwill.

The lively singing put heart into me, but it was when the choir rose for their anthem that everything tumbled into perspective. Though later I went farther afield, I think there was never a meeting in which I was involved where I was more rapidly renewed in my own spirit.

Megan occupied a place in the front row of the choir's gallery. The conductor beckoned her forward a couple of paces as the accompanist found his opening chords. Then came a clear revelation. I can rate it no less. The chosen song was a beautiful setting of Isaiah's famous prophetic assurance - 'Thou wilt keep him in perfect peace whose mind is stayed on Thee.'

The main body of the choir took the lower key and came out with the first three notes in subdued harmony. Then followed Megan's glorious soprano with the same words, rising clear as a bell, on and up to the dome of that high building, in a beautiful, echoing descant that soared over and above all the rest. I watched her spellbound from my vantage point on the platform. Her whole demeanor had changed from that of the shrinking, protesting girl whom I first encountered. Her eyes, unwavering, followed the choirmaster's baton. Gone now every trace of tears and mortification, the reddened cheeks, the petulant mouth. The devitalizing debacle of the pastor's pickles fell away into the meaningless past.

That Megan should be both the instrument of my deflation and the harbinger of the glorious exhilaration was more than a coincidence. It came from Isaiah's God and mine, and I felt no reluctance as I got to my feet, climbed into the pulpit and read my text:

> *The preaching of the cross is to them that perish foolishness, but unto us which are saved it is the power of God... God hath chosen the foolish things of the world to confound the wise; and God hath chosen the weak things of the world to confound the things which are mighty!*

I don't know how my audience reacted, but for me the words leapt from the page with convincing authority.

CHAPTER 15

Sweet Chiming Bells

'IT'S NICE of you to ask me,' I told Florence, one of our Crusader choir girls, when invited to be her bridesmaid at her Christmas wedding, 'But what about your sister?'

'Oh! Vi!' she exclaimed, then added swiftly, 'No... no I couldn't. Anyway – she wouldn't.'

Recalling what I could from occasional glimpses of Vi, I understood the bride's hesitation. None of Florence's family shared her interests in the church, Vi least of all. They put it down to a weakness on Florence's part that did her no harm, and were only mildly surprised that she was about to marry a minister, a widower in his thirties with a child from his first sadly brief marriage. But it was the contrast in the two sisters which made Vi an unlikely candidate to hold the bride's bouquet.

Ever since we had known Florence, all of her wardrobe had been on the plain side – what my mother called 'neat.' Her favourite colours were brown and beige, worn with nice but sensible shoes.

Occasionally I saw Vi crossing Friar Street en route for the City Centre, dressed in smart, figure-hugging, brightly coloured suits with dressy hats perched over tight curls and drooping low over her forehead, teetering past on very high heels. Lipsticked, powdered and heavily earringed, she was quite... well... noticeable.

I talked it over with my mother, though of course, now nearing eighteen, I was free to use my own discretion.

'You're not really a close friend of the bride,' Mother pointed out, 'And she's quite a bit older... but if her sister doesn't mind, you've got no problem there. Christmas is a lovely time for a wedding... I – I just hope that girl knows what she's taking on, that's all! One's own children can be quite a problem – but handling somebody else's, that's another thing. Florence does seem a bit... well... frail. I'd have thought the minister would have wanted somebody with a more sturdy... er... constitution...' Her voice trailed off uncertainly.

I felt a little disconcerted. I had not given thought to the weight of Florence's future responsibilities. Undoubtedly my mother's own experience of family life coloured her thoughts. She herself had been delicate in the two or three years before she married my father.

'I hardly see how I can refuse,' I said, 'She is so pleased and flattered about it all. I couldn't be a wet blanket – and obviously her sister wouldn't be right for it...' On that at any rate we were agreed and my mother sighed as she concluded, 'Well, she doesn't have much to lose in the way of home life.' The thought of our girl Crusaders living in incompatible surroundings always moved Mother to sympathy.

'After all,' I mused later,'one does not have to be one hundred per cent in favour of a marriage merely to attend the bride,' then chuckled to myself as I recalled the bridesmaid sister of a girl in my office who had resolved her reservations by running off with the groom six days before the wedding! Fortunately the bride had a large and helpful family who had scoured the likely haunts of the runaways and recovered the bridegroom in time for the ceremony, so beautifully planned, to continue. Fortunately there was a retinue of bridesmaids so the missing guilty one was hardly noticed...

Poor Florence had no family champions behind her, so I agreed to stand in. But when I called at their home to plan the wedding outfit, Vi answered the door and I beheld a very different Vi to the outdoor one. Tallish, almost gaunt, her skin sallow and devoid of all make-up, her hair was screwed tightly into metal curlers though it was early evening. Three curlers, like an overhanging gutter, surmounted the twin arches of her plucked eyebrows. A cigarette (I instinctively thought of it as a 'fag') drooped from one side of her rigid mouth. I told her what I had come for and found myself half apologizing for taking her place. Coward that I was I could not have borne to get on the wrong side of Vi! Nor to risk any repercussions on Florence...

The fag trembled on her lower lip as she replied, 'What our Floss does is our Floss's business!' and disappeared into the nether regions.

Together on the following Saturday the bride and I took the plunge into Lamb's dress shop adjoining the Market

Hall where I had once shared my Saturdays with Kit and the farm produce stall. Florence chose a full length white dress with a cowl neckline which became her modest, almost nun-like personality. A tiny chaplet of wax orange blossom and a simple unadorned veil completed the outfit. I chose blue, long sleeved, ankle length and with a couple of frilled epaulettes over each shoulder. We found somebody to make up a blue velvet Juliet cap to match it and added a little silver trimming to team up with the small spray of diamante rhinestones at the neckline of the dress, and were all set up for Boxing Day.

At the appropriate time I reported to Florence's home, arriving simultaneously with a messenger boy bearing our two bouquets, madonna lilies for Florence and a mixed posy for me. Florence was standing in the bedroom she had shared with Vi for most of her twenty-eight years, and I was thankful she had taken everybody's good advice and preserved a calmness which overcame her natural nervousness in the face of an ordeal. Since most of her future was to lie in Wales, practically all her belongings had already been packed and disposed of. Soon Vi would have the room to herself and judging by the jars and potions on hand, and the overflowing chest of drawers against the far wall, Vi would not regard this day's proceedings with disfavour.

I drew the cowl neckline carefully over Florence's head and slim white shoulders, noting the fine texture of her skin and inwardly marvelled that she had preserved such an aura of gentle grace over these past years against such an alien background as this seemed to be.

Now, my own preparations made, I slipped on the crystal pendant, the groom's gift to me, and stood at the window watching for the arrival of the uncle from Gloucestershire who would give Florence away. The aunt, who would represent her mother, would already be at the church, which unfortunately could not be our own but a neighbouring one for some reason which now escapes me.

Uncle duly arrived and gave us fresh heart for he was far more in sympathy with Florence than her immediate family could ever be, and his 'chapel' background inclined him favourably towards a parson for a nephew-in-law. A full ten minutes earlier than expected the taxi drew up outside.

Uncle went down to keep the driver occupied for a few minutes, not because we weren't ready, but for the look of

the thing. Soon he came back upstairs, 'Fellow seems a bit
impatient,' he told us, 'He's had a rotten Christmas and
says he's not going to miss this afternoon's football match
for anybody...', so we allowed ourselves to be intimidated
into leaving earlier than intended.

Florence and Uncle settled in the back seat and I took
the one beside the driver feeling a slight twinge of anxiety
because my father had booked this transport with a garage
owner of his acquaintance. We had not yet learned the
appalling risks of being a go between... The car drew
away.

Half way to the church, the driver softly mouthed
something to me which sounded alarmingly like '...couldn't
find the bridegroom.' I sat quite still clutching my posy in
my lap. I hadn't heard aright, of course! He would have
taken the groom first, as arranged by my father. Or...
was he joking? I stole a sidelong glance and in the mirror
above us caught sight of the bride looking serene and
unusually tranquil. I must have imagined what the driver
said... it couldn't be... not with everything going so well
and Florence so nice and calm.

But the unease persisted and increased when he gave
me a nudge and raised questioning eyebrows in my
direction. Trying to sound casual, I asked in a low voice,
'You... you did the first journey alright, of course?'

'No...', he ground out, still sideways on, '... wasn't
there – no reply – folks next door said they'd gone away!'

'O, Lord,' I said, and truly meant no disrespect, 'What
shall we do?'

My breath began to play peculiar tricks. We were fast
approaching the church. I glanced at my watch. We were
still early. 'Drive around the block, please,' I urged the
driver and got a startled enquiry from the back seat as we
swept past the door outside which an elderly verger was
standing. 'We're a bit early,' I said over my shoulder, and
noticed my own voice sounding unfamiliar. Florence and
Uncle relaxed again, only slightly perturbed, and I gazed
fixedly at the swiftly vanishing shop windows dappled with
a weak December sun. All too soon we were back. We
couldn't go on driving indefinitely – somebody must make
enquiries... but who... how... without arousing panic,
especially as it might all be some awful mistake anyway...
Florence was a little anaemic and had been known to faint
under stress!

We pulled up and as the driver crossed in front to open

my door I spoke over my shoulder again, 'Just hold on a
moment, will you – while we make sure everything's ready.
Let me go first.' As I stepped out, and the car door
closed, I turned to the driver, 'Maybe he's got here
before us... somehow...' I said, 'For goodness sake – go
and ask the verger!' I followed the driver across to the
door and saw them both disappear inside.

As I reached the vestibule the driver met me, 'Can't
make any ˌsense out of him,' he said, 'I don't think he can
hear!' By now the man was grasping the handle of the
door leading on into the church, ready to fulfil his normal
routine and signal to the organist the moment the bride
reached the vestibule. I glanced outside and saw that
Florence and Uncle had emerged and, her arm in his, were
approaching us at a dignified pace. Any moment the old
man would see her, give the nod and we would be regaled
with the opening bars of 'Here comes the Bride.' Gone now
my half formed plan to keep the bride in the car until the
mystery was solved. As she reached us, the verger half
opened the communicating door before I could push it to,
but at least I got his attention.

'Listen,' I implored him, 'Do you know if the
bridegroom is there?' Florence stared at me incredulously.

'Bridegroom? Bridegroom?' he queried, 'Well, he'll be in
there won't he?' and dismissed the subject as if a
bridegroom were an optional extra! Through the part open
door I glimpsed a fair sized congregation with several
heads turning in our direction. I pushed it to again and
throwing caution to the winds had to say, 'Please go down
to the front and make sure he's there!'

'I'll go and see,' he said at last, and disappeared inside
the church.

'There's been a problem,' I told Florence, who was now
white as the gown she wore. 'He was not at the house
when the taxi man went, or so the man says.' I turned to
make sure the driver had not abandoned us. 'Don't go
away, whatever you do – you shouldn't have got us here
in this situation,' I added, seeing that he looked all set to
refuse my plea. 'You should have told us before we
started out!'

Now the verger returned and shook his head. Florence
gave a little cry and Uncle moved nearer to her. I looked
wildly round for refuge and glimpsed a door behind us, at
the rear of the vestibule. This must be the vestry I
thought, and shot an enquiry at the verger.

'No - oh no! it's the... it's the... aah... you know,'
he gasped feebly.

This was no time for refinement.

'We must slip out of sight for a moment,' I said,
propelled Florence inside and found a cobwebbed, dingy
w.c. occupied solely by two brooms and a can of
disinfectant. 'I'll be back in a minute,' I promised the now
tearful bride, and dashed out to the truculent taxi man.

'Look here - it's not my fault,' he defended himself,
'Don't blame me - if you ask me, he's scarpered!'

'But he wouldn't!' I said. 'He... he couldn't!'

'How do you know?' the driver demanded, now becoming
heated.

'Because he's... not that sort,' I faltered, and
wondered - even as I said it - how I could be so sure?
People did strange things under stress. I had never in my
entire life met an absconding bridegroom, so how should I
know what sort they were?

Panic began to grip me, but I rallied. 'He's a minister!'
I told the driver, 'He wouldn't do such a thing.'

'Parsons do funny things sometimes,' he retorted, 'Look
at the Rector of Stiffkey!'

I had not the slightest desire to look at the Rector of
Stiffkey, though I knew from the popular press that
thousands paid good money to do so, on the beach at
Skegness, with him sitting in a barrel, scantily clothed. 'I
suppose you went to the right address?' I asked.

'Look here,' he demanded, 'That's what it says - No 29
Northfield Street - and the place was empty. What was I
supposed to do about it?'

Suddenly I realized the mistake.

'You should have gone to 49!' I cried, 'Please dash
back. See if he's still there!'

As his engine sprang to life, I heard the patter of
running foot-steps and saw - before anything else - a pair
of grey spats approaching at a fast trot. The missing
groom had finally despaired of the taxi and covered the
distance on foot, his best man a close second. Oh the
relief! I sped inside, ahead of the two men, in the high
heeled white shoes which I had painted silver.

As groom and friend passed through the intervening
door I retrieved Florence from the broom cupboard, gave
her a swift brush off with my gloved hand, and lined up
behind her. The door opened and the organ swung into
the familiar 'Here comes...' as we sailed in.

Moments later we found voice for the opening hymn and I looked with affection on verse 4:

Frail Children of dust, and feeble as frail;
In Thee do we trust - nor find Thee to fail...

My, oh my! This leaves little excuse for panic. All the same, the bridesmaid's role was not quite the pushover I had judged it to be!

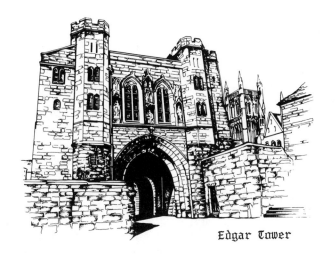

Edgar Tower

CHAPTER 16

The Hamilton Letter

HALF WAY THROUGH the nineteen thirties, following the glorious summer of George V's Silver Jubilee, it seemed that the recession was itself receding. Trade in our area picked up and my father opened a branch shop in Sidbury - which was actually a continuation of our familiar Friar Street. My grandfather's premises lay half way between our own two shops, a very convenient arrangement.

Now we were living again in the heart of the city, for the Sidbury premises provided four bedrooms as well as living quarters - an unaccustomed luxury, though scarcely more than our needs for we were eight in family. Jean, the baby, was nearing school age and our mother undertook management of the new shop in between housekeeping. She really was very good at it and we did get an interesting diversity of goods in our shop.

A narrow strip of garden at the rear provided outdoor recreation and nine-year-old Edgar had the optimism to invest in seed packets from a nearby shop, unaware of the poorness of the soil. Gazing down inscrutably upon his efforts was the stone figure of the 10th century king who bore the same name. The statue held pride of place above the archway which formed the rear entrance to the Cathedral, known as Edgar Tower, which lay a little to the rear of our shop. The king was flanked on either side by his two queens Elfrida and Elflida, so I had been told. Looking up, as I often did before passing beneath them en route to the riverside, I could not help reflecting what a happy coincidence was the similarity of their two names should the king have developed the habit of murmuring endearments in his sleep...

A portion of our rear garden was claimed by twelve-year-old Muriel, who invested in a little family of ducklings. She took pride in personally superintending their bathing lessons in the tin bath which had come into our shop with a job lot from Worcester's nearest saleroom.

The only other member of the family still at school was Ernest, taking a two year course in engineering subjects at the local 'Tec', though he appeared to have little enthusiasm for it. It almost seemed that he had again lost his way, for he was withdrawn and nobody seemed able to point his way to a career or any other direction in life which could bring him fulfilment. It troubled our mother and she sought advice.

'I don't think he's all that well, our Kate...' mused Aunt Alice, recalling her anxieties over her son Trevor. Aunt Trudie, who had a soft spot for Ernest (she had no son of her own), felt he was too pale, even allowing for the fair skin of the light-auburn-haired. Yet only occasional bouts of sickness, weakness and high temperature ensued, such as the time when, in restless fever, he refused all other drinks but expressed a longing for water from St Ann's Well at Malvern.

Fortunately our father had invested in a secondhand car. He, Edgar and I, armed with several containers of various shapes and sizes set off for the well, eight miles away. As we chugged along I thought bemusedly of the 'three mighty men' who broke through the cordon of Philistines surrounding King David in the Cave of Adullam, and succeeded in bringing him water from the well outside Bethlehem for which he had expressed a longing - at the risk of their lives!

The comparison was ridiculous of course, though let it be said that one Malvern spring is known also as the Holy Well. Today the Queen of England travels nowhere in the wide world without her supply of 'Malvern Water'. Ernest was nothing if not discriminating!

Naomi, my 'almost twin' sister had found a job in the gloving industry for which our city had a high reputation for many years, so it was a busy family with diverse interests which settled in Sidbury in 1936 and turned the old three storey shop premises into a family home. I think all of us were glad to be back in the heart of the city, despite our neighbouring premises being occupied by an undertaker. His cheerful, rubicund features did much to offset the gloom of his profession, but with such a neighbour it was inevitable that my imagination rolled back to Sidbury's past.

Facing our shop, on the opposite side of the busy road, was Danesbury House, site of Mrs Henry Wood's childhood. This was the area she found so conducive to her lively imagination, as did the Edwardian novelist, Florence Barclay. Though she spent only a few months in our city, whilst her parson father took temporary charge of a local church, it left a lasting impression on her seven-year-old mind.

Florence's parents brought her into the Cathedral hoping she would be inspired by the pure treble voices of the choir scholars, provided by the King's School, and so would pitch her voice an octave or so higher than the unusally deep contralto she used. But the child was more taken with the venerable atmosphere and ancient stone which had then been standing for eight hundred years. She looked up at the high pillars, particularly those in the crypt area, and pictured an imaginary labyrinth of underground passages extending even beyond the stone walls which bounded the Cathedral. These were to form the back-drop for her historical novel set in the period of the Third Crusade and featuring England's celebrated Crusader King, Richard the Lion Heart. She wrote it more than thirty years later and called it 'The White Ladies of Worcester.'

In the closing years of her life, which must have coincided with the opening ones of mine, she returned to our city for performances of the Three Choirs Festival. In all of her much travelled, adventurous and talented life, she enjoyed few things as she enjoyed her return to Worcester for the 1920 Festival. Her daughter was later to say:

'The setting of the beautiful cathedral which she loved so much (both on account of its associations with her childhood and with her book) enormously enhanced for her the beauty of the music which, in that atmosphere of worship, in that setting of Gothic grandeur, expressed the full religious depth and spiritual delicacy put into it by the composer.'

Returning home to Surrey, Mrs Barclay described herself as 'moved beyond words' by 'The Dream of Gerontius,' yet went through all the score with shining eyes until tears sprang to her eyes as she recalled the stirring chorus 'Go forth upon thy journey Christian soul!' Lover of music all her life, she declared Elgar's to be a revelation, 'The Apostles even more than Gerontius', because 'the one is a dream – the imaginary dream of a mortal, but the other is true – taken from the inspired Word of God.'

Florence had always attended the Handel Festival, but suddenly exclaimed to her family 'Why do they have this great orchestra and chorus, this great hall, and give three days to the music of a dead German when we have in our midst a far greater composer, a living genius, in Worcester!' It was an enormous compliment to one of our own citizens, the more gratifying because Kit had now progressed beyond her Methodist Choir and their lively concerts to become a member of the Festival Choral Society. In her black dress and demure black lace head covering, she was making her modest contribution to our city's culture by singing under the baton of Sir Ivor Atkins, Elgar's close friend, at this, Europe's oldest music festival.

Though not well versed in arts and crafts, I took pleasure in my city's prestige, enhanced as it was by the Worcester Royal Porcelain works which was producing beautiful china a mere stone's throw from our shop. Occasionally Father was able to purchase some secondhand and we possessed it for a while before surrendering it to some affluent customer. The tea and dinnerware was beautiful, gracing many a palatial function (our city always presented it to members of our own Royal Family to commemorate visits or celebrate a royal wedding), but it was the beautifully modelled figures which entranced us. Dorothy Doughty's birds held pride of place for me, and after that the lovely, colourful plates and placques displaying fruit in its prime.

The Porcelain Works had been granted its title of 'royal' by King George III who had been impressed by the delicacy and beauty of its wares when he visited Worcester for The Three Choirs Festival and stayed overnight in the nearby Bishop's Palace. It had always troubled me that we had invited Germans to come and rule over us, but seeing that Germany produced beautiful porcelain also (at Dresden), it was gratifying that King George recognized ours and granted the patent.

But Sidbury's connection with royalty went back much further and more closely with the Stuarts. On the opposite side of the road to our shop was The Commandery in which the Worcester Press of Littlebury & Co. was then housed. For me this building was the richest of all in historical association.

It marks the old City boundary, and the spot where we lived and traded would have come just within the City gate through which Charles Stuart scrambled unceremoniously across an overturned haycart on the day of his defeat in the Battle of Worcester. Roundheads swarmed up from the south in hot pursuit and were only slightly delayed by their efforts to thrust away the impeding haycart. However Charles had been thrown on to the back of a freshly saddled horse by one William Bagnall, a thoughtful Sidbury trader, and sped on through Sidbury and Friar Street to reach the Cornmarket.

Here he sprang down and hurtled inside the large corner house where he had spent the previous night, and which now proudly bears his name. Not pausing for so much as a farewell wave to his host, Squire Berkeley, he made his escape through the rear door and fled north to Boscobel and eventual refuge in France, while the Roundheads were searching the Berkeley house.

Left behind to face the music though was Charles'

Commander-in-Chief, the Scottish Duke of Hamilton with the remnants of his ten thousand Scots and two thousand English troops. He had been heavily outnumbered by Cromwell's army and undermined by internal strife between the English and the Scots. Two of his own officers were utterly incompatible in temperament, the one being dour and forbidding, while the other was a popular, jesting fellow - and their unhappy fate was that they were obliged to share a cell with each other in captivity!

Regrettably, the last straw for the ill-fated Duke was the betrayal by a Worcester citizen, a tailor named Guyes. By sneaking out of the city at nightfall and warning Cromwell, he ruined the Royalist plan of intercepting the Roundheads at our city's southern boundary with a surprise attack, disguised as ordinary citizens by wearing innocent-looking shirts over their armour.

One wonders how the tailor got his prior knowledge? It is unlikely that the plan was common knowledge. Could it be that he got a bumper rush order for outsize shirts? If so, what a shabby way to treat one's clients - and how unbecoming to the respectable profession of bespoke tailoring! His behaviour was entirely contrary to the principles of normal Worcester citizens who, next day, expressed their opinion by summarily disposing of the hapless tailor on makeshift gallows, before he had time to benefit from the influx of new prospective customers.

But, outshining all other consequences of that sad day in 1651, was the marvellous bearing of that gallant Scottish Commander under adversity. He defended Sidbury Gate as long as was humanly possible while giving the King (he had been proclaimed Charles II from our Guildhall steps) his chance of escaping to freedom. Then, as the blood of both sides mingled on the slopes of what became significantly known as Red Hill, the Duke was mortally wounded. He was carried into the Royalist headquarters - the Commandery which had once been a hospital under St Wulstan. Perhaps something of that ancient piety lingered still, for during the five traumatic days whilst his life blood ebbed away the Duke summoned strength to pen one of the most beautiful farewell letters of all time.

Sadly it cannot have reached Lady Hamilton, but has been preserved in the room where it was written -

Dear Heart
You know that I have long been labouring, though in

great weakness, to be prepared against this Expected Change, and I thank my God I find Comfort in it, in this my day of Tryal; for my body is not more weakened by my wounds than I find my spirit Comforted and Supported by the infinite Mercies and great love of my Blessed Redeemer, who will be with me to the end and in the end.

I am not able to say much more to you. The Lord preserve you under your Tryals and sanctifie the use of them to the Comfort of your Soul.

I will not so much as in a Letter divide my dear Nieces and you; The Lord grant you may be constant Comforts to one another in this Life, and send you all Eternal Happiness with your Saviour in the Life to come; to both of your cares I recommend my poor Children. Let your great work be to make them early acquainted with God, and their Duties to Him, and though they may suffer many wants before their Removal from hence, yet they will find an inexhaustible Treasure in the Love of Christ. May the Comforts of the Blessed Spirit be ever near you in all your Straits and Difficulties, and suffer not the least repining to enter into any of your Hearts for His Dispensations towards me, for His Mercies have been infinitely above His Justice in the whole pilgrimage of,

Dear Heart,

Your Own, **Hamilton.**

Ye Commanderie, Worcester.   *September 8, 1651.*

Inside The Commandery
The Great Hall

I read the letter many times after discovering it in the brochure produced by The Worcester Press. Penned under the heavy cloud of an apparent defeat, an unfulfilled vision, a lost cause, yet written without rancour or recrimination, the Duke's words were to recur to me in the following year with a strong note of poignancy, and with some personal significance.

Muriel with the Ducklings

CHAPTER 17

March Winds

ON A WINDY, overcast morning in the following February, as I prepared to dash off to the office, my father intercepted me.

'Your mother is unwell. I have to go for the doctor. He'd better see Muriel again, too. She's making no progress at all.'

His manner was fairly non-commital, as was his way, but I agreed to take a hot drink to both before leaving. The tray ready, I called first on my sister who greeted me and the Ovaltine with scant enthusiasm.

'Where's Mom?' she asked.

'Not well, I hear,' I answered, depositing the first cup. 'I'm on my way to see what's wrong.' I got a faint smile in return and left Muriel, hoping the doctor would come up with some better solution to the unusual listlessness and languor which seemed to have overtaken this normally lively child.

'It's probably her age,' he had told us the month before. 'Make a fuss of her and let her take it easy for a few weeks.'

Without protest she had relinquished her current activities which included rehearsals for a charity concert. Kit had become very friendly with the organizer, her own rich voice contributing largely to his programmes, and her Methodist Choir experience to coaxing others with sympathetic piano accompaniment. Hedley was a friendly, enterprising fellow who extended his geniality to my own family though he soon gave up Naomi and myself as being too narrow-minded to be of use to him.

However, he developed a great affection for thirteen-year-old Muriel and rather surprisingly our mother (torn between pride in her child's accomplishments and her distrust of theatricals) yielded to persuasion that Muriel should join his party with a song, dance and acrobatic technique. She was talented and made a number of successful appearances over the next year. Small, dainty and with an elfin smile she charmed everyone, and the concert party organizer was more than a little in love with her. Muriel had earned the nickname of 'Smiler' but our Grandfather Lawrence called her 'my birthday girl' because she had been born on December 13th too. It was the day which had almost cost my mother her life, at the time when this tale opened.

When I reached my mother's room with the remaining cup, I approached the bedside cheerily enough, then thrust the tray on one side and fell on my knees beside her. She was desperately gripping the sheets but making no sound. Her face was the colour of chalk and only her dark eyes alight with... was it fear? Or some wordless plea for help?

I knew at once that since my father left her there must have been a change for the worse. Swallowing hard, my mother succeeded in gasping a few words: 'a... a haemorrhage... I think,' was all she could manage.

It was a crisis and I was alone. Despite my 'hot gospel' background I had always been diffident about praying audibly, even about health or healing, for I felt there were mysteries and qualifications which were best left to those who saw their objectives more clearly. But this was no time to indulge in embarrassment or to study protocol -

without swift aid there might be only one patient in the house by the time our doctor arrived.

So I stretched out my hands upon the form clenched beneath the bedclothes and began to pour out an entreaty. Almost immediately I heard the sound of my own voice, yet the words were not of my choosing! It was an instinctive, unsought, spontaneous example of the mysterious glossalia - the strange power of speaking or praying in an untaught language.

I had known of this for several years. It was part of the Welsh Revival from which our movement had sprung. Some of the folk in our church (known familiarly as 'pentecostals') eagerly desired the charismatic phenomena which was first borne along on the wings of the rushing mighty wind that filled the house in Jerusalem in AD 33. Once, in a moment of rare ecstasy, I had experienced something of a like nature, but in the light of day and of my father's cautious counsel, I had not sought to pursue it. My mother's eager zeal had seen this as the power of the Holy Spirit, which is no doubt why I felt at that critical moment, a complete lack of inhibition in her sick room.

I opened my eyes with a sense of feeling spent, yet fulfilled. My mother's colour was coming back and she gripped my wrist reassuringly. The moment of danger had passed. Speaking of it later, she said she felt life ebbing away before I came into the room, had felt too weak to call for help and was unable to express her dilemma by the time I reached her side. The haemorrhage ceased and her strength began its slow return. Though I did not know it, she had lost her seventh child.

But before the day was out an ambulance stood at our door. My little sister, wrapped in blankets, was driven off to Worcester Royal Infirmary for examination and tests. Whilst my mother was recovering, my father and I did the hospital visiting and awaited reports in the hope that our small, unwilling patient would not long be subjected to the hospital routine. 'I'm so tired of it,' she said wearily on Saturday afternoon a week later, 'I don't want to be bothered with all this,' indicating the equipment at hand. 'I just want to come home and see Mom.'

'I'll go and see the Sister,' I offered her, 'and I'll get a couple of weeks off if we can have you home - that is, unless you need some special treatment...' My firm had been very helpful in the past couple of weeks regarding time off and I approached the Ward Sister with some confidence. My father was already there.

'You may take her home if that is your wish,' she said, more gently than was her usual manner of address.

I was surprised at the easy victory and said, 'Oh - good!'

She glanced at me briefly. 'Not really,' she said as she turned away, 'Your father is waiting to see the doctor, when the other visitors have gone.'

Emerging from that interview my father's face was very set and he despatched me on home.

'But what's the news?' I asked, 'Mom will want to know.'

I'll tell her all about it later,' he replied, 'For the moment I want to go to the shop in Friar Street. The news... it's not very good.' He hurried away and I made my own way by a more direct route to Sidbury. Knowing my father's capacity for understatement, I felt his few words sounded ominous.

I reached home and let myself in. Mother, now convalescent, turned an enquiring head against the wingback of her fireside chair. 'Not much news yet,' I said carefully, 'but Muriel will be home soon - tomorrow I think.'

'Well - that's all the news I want,' exclaimed Mother, and the tension left her shoulders. 'Now draw up your chair. Naomi's got tea ready.'

They plied me with mustard and cress served with thinly sliced brown bread and Danish butter. Somehow I got some of it down, but - to the end of my life I think - mustard and cress will taste like cooled ashes. I firmly refused the strawberry jam and seed cake.

During the night my father's careful control deserted him and obliged him to tell my mother that their fourth child was soon to die.

During the next few days I got leave from the office, and our family - Lawrences and Hardwicks - rallied round with deep concern and kindness.

'What about Switzerland?' asked Uncle Sidney gruffly, I'll pay - we'll fly her out - if it will do any good, to save our little Mu.' We appreciated the offer the more, knowing him to be a practical businessman who had built up his resources by hard work. He was not one given to profligate expenditure, and few people as yet travelled by air. Often he had teased me, with his glass of wine in hand, claiming to be my 'wicked uncle'. The day he offered Switzerland there was no twinkle in his eye... but I liked him just the same.

'Now then,' counselled our Great Aunt Kate from Malvern in her quick, bird-like way, 'Don't let yourselves get downhearted. You're a good chapel-going lot, and I'm sure things will turn out for the best...' Our nice plump Aunt Mabel came down from Birmingham, and her maternal, comforting bulk was somehow reassuring. Then came Aunt Alice with her unflappable demeanor. Kit was her usual feeling, sympathetic self, living with us all the hopes and fears that alternated. Flowers, fruit and goodwill flowed in with the prayers and encouragement of our church friends and others.

My mother, even on hearing that X-rays revealed the advanced disease of her child's lungs, clung desperately to the hope and faith inspired by the Divine Healing campaign eight years earlier and possibly reinforced by her own recent experience through me. Not unnaturally she looked for a stimulus to her own faith in those around her, for we had always understood that faith was a significant factor in the prayer for healing.

My father was predominantly practical in his outlook. He was fully aware of the mysterious events that had occurred on the Day of Pentecost and at the turn of the century in South Wales, but there were highly respected Christian believers (many in the Plymouth Brethren assembly for which he held great affection) who contended that the events then manifested were confined to the Early Church period. Yet history revealed that the ministry of the miraculous with its supernatural energies runs like a combustible fuse through the long story of the church and flares up at intervals into a conflagration which cannot be ignored.

So what of the here and now? The immediate apalling need?

Healing ministry was no longer an interesting debating point. It was the only possible source of hope. My mother looked at my father, desperately anxious for his support. He came across, and quoted a reference to the old patriarch Abraham (Weymouth's translation of Romans 4: 18): 'Under hopeless circumstances he hopefully believed.' It was as far as he could go.

For myself, I was conscious that I had inherited more of my father's nature than my mother's and was influenced

by my deeper affection for him. Yet I recognized in my
mother a greater stature in spiritual things. It betrayed
itself in other ways, not merely in this matter of desperate
hope. As day succeeded day, I watched keenly for every
sign of God's good grace.

* * * * *

'We're not going to a funeral, Kath!'

Three weeks after her return home from hospital, my
sister's spirited rebuke cut across my thoughts, and with
a start I realized how slowly I was brushing the pretty,
fair hair that fell against the pillow as Muriel half lay, half
crouched on one elbow above it. Tenderness and
apprehension had combined to produce something of the
melancholy which we had determined to submerge, and had
slowed my movements.

'Oh... sorry!' I apologized with a wry smile. I
continued at a brisker pace, then - as Muriel's words
re-echoed in my mind - my heart gave a hopeful leap!
Could it be that this exasperated exclamation was fraught
with meaning? Even perhaps... prophetical? And the very
humanity of my sister's impatience seemed somehow to draw
her back from the shadows to the solid earth with which
we were more familiar. My heart high with hope, I thought
I detected a new strength in the pretty features and went
to report to the family downstairs.

Towards lunchtime Muriel announced that she would like
to come downstairs into the living room after tea, to listen
with us to the latest instalment of 'The Count of Monte
Cristo' on radio. Also, she fancied some celery for tea!

Gladly we busied ourselves with preparations, arranging
a couch beside the hearth, looking out warm wrappers and
deputing some strong body to carry her down at the right
time. While she rested for the afternoon, I set off in
search of the requested celery. It so happened this was
not an easy task at that time, but I got out my cycle and
felt I could ride to Land's End if need be.

Returning, I found we had a visitor, Muriel's
headmistress from the school around the corner, and
Muriel was sleeping despite the murmur of voices at her
bedside. Then came the sound of the sleeper's own voice,
softly, almost like a sighing in the wind, and I caught
only two or three words: '...thy going out... thy coming
in...'

The headmistress prepared to leave, but leaned closer as the low voice came again. 'Why - it's the hundred and twenty first psalm,' she breathed, 'We taught it... at school.'

My mother stooped over the bed, took a handkerchief and wiped something from the sleeper's face. She looked up at me, her eyes darker with apprehension. The headmistress moved quietly towards the door and mechanically I accompanied her to see her out. As her dignified, upright form disappeared into the street I seemed to hear the drone of forty dispirited voices in an old classroom where the red-painted fire escape obscured the view from the far window:

Shall I have naught that is fair, said he?
Naught but the bearded grain...?

The words of the Reaper. I sped back up the twisting stairway again and heard once more the gentle voice: 'The Lord... shall preserve... thy going out and thy coming in... from this time forth... even for evermore...'

At seven o'clock, when the beautiful voice of Terence de Marney broke into a thousand homes around us, our own radio was silent. We had no appetite for the drama of Jean Valjean's misfortunes. The little blithe spirit had flown beyond hearing.

I awoke on the following morning with a feeling of heaviness in my chest, and lay quite still as consciousness fully returned. I did not wish to arouse others too soon to meet this new day. Two or three words tumbled over and over in my mind, and I knew they came from my own heart and held a note of protest, almost of reproach: 'But... we trusted! we trusted...' My breath came and went shallowly as I thought of the still pretty, composed little face in the room across the landing. The words came again: '... but we trusted.'

Again I knew that this protest came from my own heart, yet I felt no fear or guilt as I dwelled on the words. Then, quite spontaneously they fell into context, almost as if I had seen the words flicker and clarify on a screen. 'But we trusted it had been He which should have redeemed Israel...'

Quite soon Easter would be upon us, and thousands would recall as I did then, the two dispirited disciples who traversed the eight miles from Calvary to Emmaus. They too had known what it was to have hope and high endeavour die within them. They had been drawn to a Man of wisdom and power who seemed to point them to a horizon far beyond the limited landscape of their immediate environment. They had felt His charisma, glimpsed His miraculous power, shared His compassion and yet – had seen Him die the death of a common felon.

So they turned back from Olivet... Gethsemene... Calvary, and trod their way with heavy footsteps, back home to the everyday... the coming to terms and the unknown future. The adventure was over. A dream had faded. Where now could they look for a purpose in life?

But on the way to Emmaus they were joined by One whom, though they did not recognize Him then, held the key to the past and the future. And in turning that key the present... the overcast, perplexing present... was circled by a rainbow.

As we moved slowly along Sidbury three days later, behind the flower-laden casket, my father hummed a few bars of an old hymn and familiarity with it identified the refrain...

He knows... He knows...
And tempers every wind that blows.

My mother laid her hand upon his, though she – of greater faith – could not give voice to her thoughts. We passed the Commandery gates where the king's champion had succumbed to mortal wounds, had expended his failing strengh on testifying to an immortal victory and a kingdom yet to come, and who had found the grace to write:

Suffer not the least repining... His Mercies have
been infinitely above His Justice.

With the privilege of hindsight I took comfort in the knowledge that after the weakness, the pain and the loss, the rejected King returned to claim his throne, his crown and his sceptre. There had come Another Day.

CHAPTER 18

Laughing with Sarah

THE TRAIN FILLED rapidly as it sped through the Midlands into the north of England. Bank holiday crowds returning from the day's jaunts converged into passenger coaches from all directions, shuffling along in search of seats. From my own seat, adjoining the corridor, I kept a wary eye on my luggage. Because the overhead rack was so narrow, it had not been possible to balance the 'travelling wardrobe' up there without a distinct risk of it descending, when the train lurched to a stop, upon my own head or that of some other unfortunate. When I had been offered my present seat, I had been obliged to leave the trunk just outside the doorway and so long as I could keep the door open a few inches I could ensure its safety. Nobody had actually stumbled over it!

I was beginning to regret the impulse which had made

me borrow this recent acquisition from among my father's
saleroom treasures, but when packing I had noticed the
'portmanteau' fitted with clothes hangers and metal rail on
which the garments could be draped wardrobe style and
then dexterously folded over only once. On reflection I
really should have taken
advice and had the luggage
sent in advance. Was I too
distrusting?   Or   over -
possessive about my things?
But this was war-time Britain,
rail schedules sometimes went
haywire,   and   the   risk   of
arriving at a honeymoon hotel
to   find   no   luggage   was   a
disconcerting prospect.

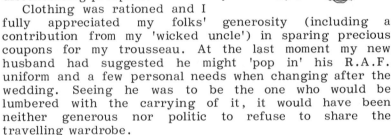

    Clothing was rationed and I
fully   appreciated   my   folks'   generosity   (including   a
contribution from my 'wicked uncle') in sparing precious
coupons for my trousseau. At the last moment my new
husband had suggested he might 'pop in' his R.A.F.
uniform and a few personal needs when changing after the
wedding. Seeing he was to be the one who would be
lumbered with the carrying of it, it would have been
neither generous nor politic to refuse to share the
travelling wardrobe.

    Petrol was rationed so we were reluctantly obliged to
use public transport for this journey to the Lake District,
but once seated in the knowledge that the hassle of
changing trains was over, the rhythm of the turning
wheels and the rocking motion of the speeding train was
comforting. As the midsummer daylight faded I looked
across to the flying fields and hedgerows and to the arc of
the setting sun framing distant hills. The words of our
wedding hymn, and particularly the musical tenor of my
father's voice as he stood on my right, reiterated in my
mind...

Heaven above is softer blue,
*   Earth around is sweeter green,*
* Something lives in every hue*
*   Christless eyes have never seen...*

    The events of this crowded Whit Monday flitted through
my thoughts. I had no regrets for choosing the building

that had once been The Apollo Cinema (alias the Flea Pit) for my wedding, though in my city of many spires I could have chosen a more salubrious setting. But what the building lacked in mystique had been compensated for by the atmosphere of warmth and affection with which the wedding preparations had been made. The place was filled with the fragrance of flowers. June roses and Whitsuntide bosses hung everywhere. The area where once the screen commanded rapt attention was now a combined platform and pupit where the scent of orange blossoms predominated. Friendly, smiling faces beamed over the edge of the gallery as I looked up on arrival. The Scottish minister who was the Whitsuntide Convention speaker here performed the ceremony admirably.

Three years since my sister's death had brought swift changes for the nation and for me personally. A few years after the happy, lively reopening of the Lowesmoor Chapel, which meant so much for us as a family, a quite traumatic controversy had occurred, leading to a split among its members. At first it seemed incredible, but I smiled wryly at the recollection of the wag who said:

> To dwell above with saints you love,
> O, wouldn't that be glory!
> To dwell below with saints you know
> Well... that's another story!

The bone of contention centred on the pentecostal element in the movement and in individual churches. Was it a dynamic force or a divisive factor? Not everyone wanted to be associated with those mysterious happenings on the Day of Pentecost which separated us from the mainstream of Christian communities. The movement's founder, Edward Jeffreys, despite his family's roots in the Welsh Revival, eventually pronounced against the inclusion of charismatic doctrine in our churches and issued an edict to that effect.

But this was not good enough for the pentecostal group in our church who had experienced a depth in worship which they could not now forego, and they broke away from us. Mother watched them go with reluctance. They were zealots and of such was her own indomitable spirit. But I followed my father's judgement in the dispute, though I could not deny that I had myself experienced the touch of pentecostal fire. My father and the young pastor he liked so well, agonized together over the final break, for it left the church quite seriously diminished. As the minister paced round and round our (fortunately circular) dining table, Father played soothing airs upon our little American organ annexed from his shop.

With hindsight it seemed that the Bethel Evangelistic movement grew more rapidly than did its organizational ability, and lacked something of the capacity to direct when a difficult situation arose. Subsequently Edward Jeffreys and our own pastor Anderson-Brown made a surprise decision to join the Anglican priesthood. The Bethel churches were given U.D.I.

Some remained bravely independent; others teamed up with similar movements. Perhaps the most surprising development locally was that my father (that avowed non-pentecostal) took the remaining trustee of our church to Clapham Crescent in London and handed over the Deeds of Lowesmoor Chapel to the Elim Pentecostal movement. This was ultimately to yield very good dividends, but at the time when I was sufficiently qualified and free to join the staff-cum-student body of the Bible College in Bristol, it had closed due to the realignment of the movement.

So... I never did get the chance to say 'No, John, No' in the rarefied atmosphere of the College – and I have to confess that my feelings of independence had suffered something of a jolt in two directions.

On a night of loneliness at the time of my sister's death I had walked for two hours with my personal grief and thought with some regret of the banished Local Preacher with the broad shoulders who had found consolation among the Methodists with a girl who knew more clearly where she was going. A few months earlier we had come away from a missionary meeting, laughing together over the adventures and misadventures of Irene Clark in the Belgian Congo, evangelizing on a cycle over rutted tracks.

'Will you go?' he asked, for there had been the customary appeal for recruits.

'Who knows?' I replied cautiously, for I was anxious to avoid any personal or spiritual commitment.

'Even so,' he rejoined heartily, 'You'll need somebody along to mend the punctures. Don't forget me!'

Well, I needed more than a rubber patch and adhesive on that sad night in March 1936. Though I was not in love, and knew it, I almost succumbed to the selfish impulse to recall him – influenced, perhaps unconsciously,

by the coincidence that he came from the same village as
the burly, kindly farmer who had been host to our
Brownie Pack twelve years earlier, and against whose
rough tweeds I had nestled on my first night away from
home. Does one ever quite 'grow up'?

Shortly after that night I happened to pass the tall,
depressing row of solicitors' offices in Pierpoint Street
where, on my way home from school years before, I had
felt nauseated and suffered something of an inhibition
towards marriage. Ahead I glimpsed a slim girl walking
briskly beside a trotting small boy, around four years old
I judged, dressed in a brown tweed overcoat and a jockey
cap to match. The girl glanced sideways at him as they
reached the road junction, putting out a protecting hand.
She noticed, as I then did, that one fawn sock had slipped
half way down from where it should have been. She
stooped to tug it upwards and I suddenly recognized the
profile of the pretty schoolgirl who had left us abruptly in
our closing term. In this little fellow I saw the likely
reason.

Whether it was something in the look which passed
between them or not I shall never quite know, but
something inside of me turned over with a lurch that was a
physical reality. I drew in my breath with surprise. I
must be crazy, I thought – I had fallen in love with a
four-year-old in a sloppy sock! It was out of character for
me. Maybe I was a late developer in more ways than one?
Had I been too ambitious? Over confident in my ability to
plough my own furrow?

I eventually gave notice to leave my job, thinking I
would be leaving the city for Bristol. I was at a
crossroads when my plans fell through so abruptly and
unexpectedly. I had no clear direction as to the course
ahead. I decided to mark time by taking a job as Private
Secretary to the proprietor of a Riding Academy in
Malvern and there followed a lively two years among
society completely different from any in my previous
environment or from that anticipated in the Bible College.
To my own surprise, for I knew I took a risk and had
been cautioned by Uncle Sidney 'They're not your kind of
people, Kathie,' I soon found some kind of rapport with
the peppery, ill-tempered ex-Army officer and the
delightful woman who had eloped with him to India when
only seventeen. My office was in their home and I found
that her bedside reading contrasted strangely with her

husband's Sporting Times. She cherished a copy of Mrs
Charles Cowan's *Streams in the Desert.*

Frankly, I enjoyed the complete change and having
daily use of the big green Chrysler saloon acquired from
Lady Mary Lygon of nearby Madresfield Court, who was
preparing to marry a Russian Prince. Captain Jack Hance
was on close terms with all Earl Beauchamp's family there,
and seemed to be held in affectionate awe by the society
folk and celebrities who booked in for riding courses and
horse training at The Equitation School.

As the northbound train rumbled on, my thoughts were
interrupted momentarily by a passenger who stumbled past
me en route for the corridor. Before the door slid to after
him, I hastily checked that our big suitcase was still
standing alongside. Because our compartment was so full,
my husband had been obliged to find a seat in the
opposite corner, so conversation between us was limited
and I was soon left again to my thoughts. In these brief
hours of travel, which somehow separated my old life from
the new one ahead, perhaps it was natural that my mind
ruminated on the events leading to this particular day.

How odd, I thought, how very odd that it had been the
Pentecostals whom I had not really appreciated and about
whom I still had reservations, who had generously thrown
open the doors of their church to us for our wedding
ceremony. After leaving the Lowesmoor Church they had
continued in strength, taken over the Apollo Cinema after
the friendly Evans family had called a halt to their film
enterprise, and restored the building as the Zion Chapel
for which it had been constructed. Our marriage service
had been an unusual prelude to their Whitsuntide
Convention and the warmth of their welcome was due, I
felt certain, to their affection and respect for my mother.

In view of this strange venue, it was inevitable perhaps
that my thoughts turned to Edgar Wallace who brought his
steed to Captain Hance at Malvern for training. I might
have a golden opportunity to ask him how The Green
Archer finished, for I did not have the satisfaction as a
child of seeing the last instalment at The Apollo and so
never knew for certain whether the doughty marksman
rescued the mysterious prisoner in the tower of the moated
castle. But just as the author arrived with groom and
horsebox, I was despatched to an antique shop to find a
wedding present for the Hon. Lavinia Strutt who was
about to marry the Duke of Norfolk. I had never before

had occasion to buy a present for a duke, and being
cautioned: 'For goodness sake find a bargain, Kathleen,
we're pretty nearly broke!' it was understandable that I
was too preoccupied to follow through the tale with Mr
Wallace.

It was illuminating to find the privileged Upper Crust
also beset with problems. My girlhood heroine, the aviator
Amy Johnson, came to us at a time when her sky was very
clouded following the break up of her marriage with Jim
Mollison. Sadly, she turned for some consolation to alcohol
which led to a brush with the Malvern Police. Perhaps it
was a pity she brought her own car (I ferried the pupils
who did not) for she was found to be 'over the limit' while
at the wheel. The Captain was furious when they convicted
her, and spoke roundly in her defence - but his protests
carried little weight with the sober magistrates who had
been offput by previous tirades from him.

The school came to an end with the Munich crisis of
1938. The Captain was recalled to the Army, delighted to
get back into uniform. Mrs Hance was unwell and was
despatched to her daughter, Mrs Dick Whittington, a
stockbroker's wife. 'I'm afraid you'll have to cope with it,
Child,' bid the Captain in his imperious way, and left me
to terminate the lease, sell the furniture, cancel his
judging appointments, hotel bookings, training programmes
and return the horses undergoing training. I took home
with me the most important files and the manuscript of the
book on which we had been working.

Though war was not yet declared, the Captain fully
anticipated it and left Malvern without regret. 'If it comes,
even you might get called up, Child,' he warned me, 'Try
for the Army. I'll get you posted to my unit. We might
even finish my book.'

But there was a risk to wearing khaki - flat heeled
brogues and drilling grounds! Would patriotism demand
that of me?

I had other plans, largely depending on whether the
war clouds would lift. Some months earlier I had met and
given some assistance to Dan & Gwen Walters, missionaries
to Northern India, who had offered me the chance to
return with them after their furlough. Dan felt it not
necessary, for their purpose, for me to have Bible College
training. 'Be ready,' he suggested, 'for next October...'
It was not a clear cut 'call' perhaps, but it was an
unexpected opportunity to make something significant of

my life. Could it be right for me? Would the war clouds lift to allow passage of missionary personnel?

But on September 3rd war was declared and I took a job with Berrows Newspapers which gave me an unexptected chance of entering the world of freelance journalism and of savouring the first secret pleasure of seeing my words clothed in print. The newspaper provided the natural centre for Civil Defence Communications and I was awarded three stripes and a navy uniform to look after the women's section by my newspaper boss, also the Commandant. We organized our war effort and various supporting events to inspire patriotism, in particular a citywide Wings for Victory Week which brought a large influx of R.A.F. personnel of all ranks through our door.

Yet... despite the many distractions of war and a successful career, my loyalty to the Invisible Kingdom remained the priority in my life. Most of my colleagues accepted my 'eccentricities' and my newspaper boss introduced me to the Wing Commander who was arranging the Squadronaires Concert: 'You'll never believe this, but I landed myself with a Hot Gospeller for a secretary!'

This was usually the signal for goodnatured banter, but one R.A.F. postal clerk was not offput. 'My mother was in the Salvation Army,' he said, 'So I know the drill.' It transpired that his father was one of the Black Country Bible-named descendants of an evangelist who came out of Wales to join the Wesleys. More to the point, he himself had found faith in Christ through a Salvationist preacher. Possibly being in charge of a Field Post Office provided an easy means of pursuing his suit through the mail, and a year later, when he was withdrawn from a convoy for Cyprus, we had married.

Now the train was slowing for its next stop. Passengers were groping around for their belongings. With a lurch we drew to a halt at Lancaster. Outgoing passengers were quickly replaced by others, some of them markedly unsteady on their feet. I hoped our luggage would not prove to be their undoing but the train drew off again without any apparent disaster, though it left a number of passengers standing in the corridor.

The door to our compartment was practically closed. I eased myself forward in my seat and smiled polite assurance in response to my neighbour's 'Alright Luv?' On my feet, I opened the compartment door and stepped into the corridor - just to make sure...

My heart turned over. The big suitcase had vanished!

For a few seconds I stared stupefied, then beckoned my husband to join me. 'It's gone!' I said, pointing to the empty space.

He whistled, more in amazement than dismay. 'Probably been put in the guard's van,' he said, 'He may have thought it in the way - or left behind by someone.' We found the van and scanned it eagerly, but in vain. The guard was irritable at the end of a demanding day and denied any knowledge or responsibility for taking action. I was torn between an urgent desire to traverse the train in search of our luggage, or press our suit with authority in the shape of this weary man.

'You shouldn't have left it there,' he grunted unnecessarily. I had already come to that conclusion. 'But I thought it might fall on somebody,' I protested a little feebly. My concern for humanity fell on deaf ears.

'Only one thing to do,' pronounced the guard, 'Report it at the other end.' He left us and we fell silent, each with our own thoughts. By the time we reached our destination it was nearing midnight and the train was almost empty. A last frantic search yielded no result. At Bowness the sleepy ticket-collector prepared to hurry us through the barrier and lock up for the night. He was not pleased when my husband told him of our loss. 'We were told to report it to you,' I mentioned, in support.

Wordlessly, the man unlocked a door behind him, took out a ledger and opened it to a new page. 'Alright then... name and address... and a list of the contents!'

'Are you going to do anything about it tonight?' I asked.

He bridled. 'What do you expect?' he demanded, 'I'll get on the phone in the morning.'

So we gave in our name and address and a description of the case. I had seen a tall, well built figure standing outside the station beside a station wagon and felt we could not keep our host waiting longer. He would already be mystified at our delay in emerging. 'We'll bring you a list in the morning,' I concluded, and we went out to the waiting vehicle. I was glad, in the circumstances, we had not betrayed to our hotel that we were newlyweds...

The inevitable question came: 'Where's your luggage?' and we parried it as lightheartedly as we could. 'I think it will be found,' I said, 'It's an unusually big case. They promised to send it on.'

Over the three miles to the hotel our driver, who turned out to be the hotel owner, was not very forthcoming. In preparation for the list we had promised to deliver, I cast my mind over the contents of the trunk. I hardly dared dwell on the new pretty things bought with hoarded coupons and never yet worn; the midnight blue dress, the new négligé, the apple green dressing gown which had been such a trouble to shorten... And oh! my shoes! I had travelled to London for them, to a shop off Regent Street which specialized in 'large and small sizes.' Well, the odds were very much against anyone else having use for them. Surely... they would come back... It all would. Nobody would run off with a case that size!

At the big country house where we drew up, only one light burned. Our host conducted us up the broad staircase to our room and left us. Silence reigned everywhere. Alone together for the first time in this eventful day, we sank down on the edge of the bed and regarded each other quizzically.

'D'you think he guessed about us?' I asked, and felt strangely comforted by the reply, 'No... I don't think so for a minute. You carried it off well!'

A quick tap on the door startled us. It opened a fraction and a small bundle skimmed across the room – it consisted of a very large pair of blue and white pyjamas and a small, pale green nightdress. 'Best I can do for the moment,' came our host's gruff voice, 'and there's a telegram inside – arrived this afternoon.'

He disappeared as we voiced our surprised thanks. The buff envelope was stamped 'confirmation' so we knew the contents had already been telephoned to the hotel in advance. The message was understandably brief. How much to the point it was, the sender could not have guessed:

WISHING YOU EVERY BLESSING ON YOUR
MARRIAGE TODAY STOP   ROMANS EIGHT
TWENTY EIGHT STOP

We looked at each other wordlessly. So our host knew before he met us that we were on honeymoon! As for the Scripture reference at the end of the message, we did not need to check on it – it was the classic philosophy of the Christian optimist: 'And we know that all things work together for good to them that love God...!

Something began to quiver inside me. I rolled over and buried my face in the pillow. Laughter shook me until my whole body was convulsed. A questing hand touched my shoulder and I managed a sidelong glance. My husband dropped down beside me and began to laugh with the same helpless abandon.

It was one o'clock in the morning, in a strange place filled with sleeping people we had never seen. Yet, at that moment, it seemed that from somewhere across the Pennines the sun peeped through our dormer window.

It is recorded that perfect love casts out fear. Shared laughter must come a close second.

Once, long ago, a woman laughed – at first derisively, desperately hurt in the face of an impossible prediction, of disappointed hopes and sensitive to the fear of herself becoming a laughing stock. Then, long past hope, the promise she despaired of sprang to fulfilment, and Sarah laughed again. This time it was the glorious, infectious mirth of full release.

Sarah was born too soon to read the New Testament or she would have put her finger upon Romans 8: 28. Instead, it was her destiny to contribute to the Book of Genesis and to provide a vital link in the chain of events which would inspire St Paul to write his Letter to the Romans.

Could any woman ask for greater fulfilment? And along with it came the marvellous bonus of love and laughter.

'God hath made me to laugh,' she said, 'so that all that hear shall laugh with me!'

Also from Bridge Publications:

LAUGH WITH ME

From the Severn to the Golden Horn

Kathleen Lawrence-Smith
ISBN 0 947934 08 1

Foreword by George Thomas, Viscount Tonypandy of Rhondda and former Speaker of the House of Commons.

This book, though a complete tale in itself, forms an interesting sequel to GOD HATH MADE ME TO LAUGH. It covers the years 1943 to 1963 in the writer's life as a suburban housewife and mother whose interests in the outside world are widened by her family's involvement in property development and, more particularly, in landlord-tenant relationships.

***

"It is a volume of autobiography in which there is not the slightest self-indulgent egotism. Like bright Mr Pepys, she looks outwards all the time, her eyes and thoughts keenly engaged in the life around."

"Mrs Lawrence-Smith has a happy gift of quotation which makes one recall those wonderful teachers who were around in our schools in the earlier years of this century. The author is their product."

The Bridge

"Whether she is recalling shared homes, recalcitrant workmen or an overland journey to Jerusalem, this unassuming writer turns the daily round into a vivid and often funny story. And her own Evangelical Christian commitment is as refreshingly tolerant as her attitudes to life in general."

Church Times

£4.95 from any bookseller, or by post (add 50p) from the publishers.

By the same author

The Bassano Tragedy, Kathleen Lawrence-Smith's first book, published by Pearl Books, is available from the author at the address below.

Murder is always a tragedy, and when it strikes at someone you know and love it is devastating. Reg and Grace Tomlinson were known throughout Britain for their ministry of song, their children's evangelism, their utter dedication to the call of God wherever it took them and for their engaging personalities.

Why were they, Philomena Levens and her children, all shot and killed in Bassano, 'a little town on the Prairies'? The events that preceded and ultimately brought about this bizarre tragedy on the eve of an evangelistic crusade are recorded in this book not to sensationalise a tragedy but to share the love and grace of God which is so well illustrated in the life and death of 'The Tomlinsons'.

£3.50 (including postage) from:

The Editor
Anchored Magazine
The Old Coach House
Whittington
Worcester
WR5 2RQ